AF334947

505 TELEVISION QUESTIONS

YOUR FRIENDS CAN'T ANSWER

HARRY CASTLEMAN and WALTER J. PODRAZIK

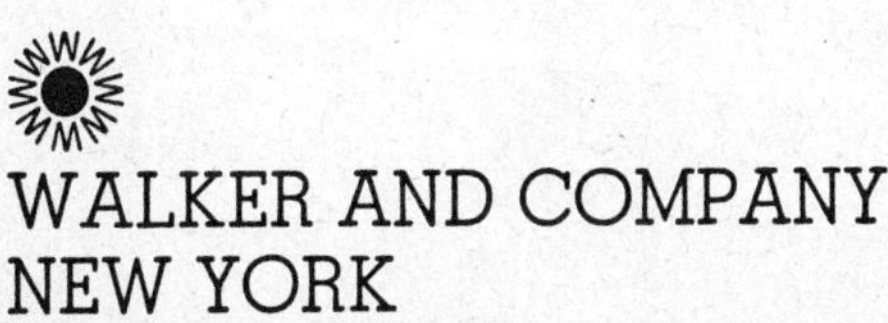

WALKER AND COMPANY
NEW YORK

Copyright © 1983 by Walter J. Podrazik and Harry Castleman

All rights reserved. No part of this book may be reproduced or transmitted in any form or by any means, electric or mechanical, including photocopying, recording, or by any information storage and retrieval system, without permission in writing from the Publisher.

First published in the United States of America in 1983 by the Walker Publishing Company, Inc.

Published simultaneously in Canada by John Wiley & Sons Canada, Limited, Rexdale, Ontario.

ISBN: 0-8027-0731-9 (cloth)
      0-8027-7210-2 (paperback)

Library of Congress Catalog Card Number: 82-40441

Printed in the United States of America

10 9 8 7 6 5 4 3 2 1

Library of Congress Cataloging in Publication Data
Castleman, Harry.
   505 television questions your friends can't answer.

   1. Television broadcasting—United States—Miscellanea.
I. Podrazik, Walter J. II. Title. III. Title: Five
hundred five television questions your friends can't answer.
PN1992.9.C37 1983   791.45   82-40441
ISBN 0-8027-0731-9
ISBN 0-8027-7210-2 (pbk.)

MIDDLE SCHOOL LIBRARY

18.274

CONTENTS

791.45
Ca3

$6.48

Econo-Clad

91281.85

INTRODUCTION

Everyone's a TV expert. After thousands of viewing hours each, how could we avoid it? We've shared comedy, drama, variety, commercial plugs, and real-life news events through the magic of the tube. Now here's an excuse to look back on it all.

Because this is a memory-jogging quiz book, we've downplayed isolated, unconnected facts in favor of more anecdotal questions. That way, even if you miss a few, the stories themselves can serve as an entertaining consolation prize.

So choose your channel and return to your favorite era—or visit another for the first time. Along the way you'll probably surprise yourself by discovering how much you remember from all your years of watching TV.

First, though, we'd like to thank: The Museum of Broadcasting in New York City for providing the opportunity for us to check obscure points firsthand; Mike Tiefenbacher for letting us test the finished manuscript on him in one marathon sitting; and friends Dean Yannias, Joe Federici, Laura Janis, Susan Novak, Bud Podrazik, David Pately, and Barbara Brown for first-draft reactions and criticisms. Above all, we'd like to thank Nicholas Schaffner and PJ Haduch for the initial suggestion and persistent follow-up.

And now forward—into the past!

Harry Castleman and Wally Podrazik

SWITCH ON/ WARM UP

Switch On/ Warm Up

1. Who shot J. R.?

2. What planet did Mork come from?

3. In *Roots: The Next Generations,* who played American Nazi leader George Lincoln Rockwell?

4. Which of Charlie's Angels were the blondes and which were the brunettes?

5. Name all the roommates and the landlords from *Three's Company.*

6. In 1975, NBC axed the peacock in favor of a new million-dollar corporate symbol. What was it?

7. What did private investigator Jim Rockford use as his combined home and office?

8. Who won ABC's "battle of the sexes" tennis match between Bobby Riggs and Billie Jean King?

9. Who was the only performer from the original *M*A*S*H* theatrical film to make the character crossover to the television series?

10. Who directed "Murder by the Book," the first entry in the regular *Columbo* series?

11. Name the American shows based on the following popular British series: *Till Death Do Us Part; Steptoe and Son;* and *Man About the House.*

12. The series *My World and Welcome to It* incorporated animated fantasy sequences based on the stories and sketches of what writer-humorist?

13. What was the "Heidi" incident?

14. Why was Chief Robert Ironside confined to a wheelchair?

15. Who really did kill Dr. Richard Kimble's wife?

16. Who did producer William Dozier choose as the dramatically hokey voice-over announcer-narrator for *Batman*?

17. Name the five passengers who set sail on the *Minnow* only to find themselves shipwrecked on *Gilligan's Island*?

18. On February 9, 1964, *The Ed Sullivan Show* opened and closed with performances by what hot new British rock group?

19. What futuristic animated cartoon program was also ABC's first color series?

20. The first televised debates between presidential candidates took place in the fall of 1960. Who were the two participants?

21. Who hosted CBS's weekly Sunday afternoon documentary program, *The Twentieth Century*?

22. Who was the executive producer, host, and frequent writer for *The Twilight Zone*?

23. What sex was the collie that played Lassie?

24. Who was a quizmaster on NBC's *The Big Surprise*, narrator for the syndicated *Biography*, and also co-host for CBS's *60 Minutes*?

25. ABC's *Sports Focus* premiered in the summer of 1957, providing the first regular network television show for what sports commentator?

26. On the original *Mickey Mouse Club,* each day of the week had a special theme. What were the five day titles?

27. In December 1954, the prime-time *Disneyland* series touched off a nationwide fad with the adventures of what Western hero?

28. One of the most popular regulars on the *Today* show in the early 1950s was J. Fred Muggs. What set him apart from the rest of the crew?

29. What event sent the ratings through the roof for the January 19, 1953, episode of *I Love Lucy?*

30. How did Edward R. Murrow demonstrate the electronic magic of live, coast-to-coast television on the 1951 premiere broadcast of his *See It Now* program?

31. In the fall of 1950, both Chico Marx and Groucho Marx hosted new prime-time network series. Name them.

32. What tall, buxom blonde was the most popular member of Jerry Lester's supporting crew on NBC's late-night *Broadway Open House?*

33. What NBC news anchor used to "hopscotch the world for headlines"?

34. What pair of "zany comics" appeared on Ed Sullivan's first *Toast of the Town* program?

35. Who was the uncrowned king of early television, whose Tuesday night variety series inspired millions to buy their first TV sets?

36. Who was the host of television's first hit children's show, DuMont's *Small Fry Club?*

37. What was the first "big budget" TV variety show, premiering in May 1946?

38. What was the first successful long-lasting commercial network television program, premiering September 29, 1944?

39. On April 30, 1939, NBC-TV covered the opening of the New York World's Fair, including an address by the first U.S. president to appear on television. Who was that?

40. Who demonstrated the world's first working television system on June 13, 1925?

ANSWERS

1. *Kristin Shepard (Mary Crosby), J. R.'s mistress and Sue Ellen's sister. A record-breaking number of viewers tuned in Dallas on the night of November 21, 1980, to learn the answer.*

2. *Mork came from the planet Ork.*

3. *Marlon Brando made a rare television appearance in the role of George Lincoln Rockwell—at quite a bit below his asking price for theatrical features such as Superman.*

4. *Jaclyn Smith (as Kelly Garrett) and Kate Jackson (as Sabrina Duncan) were the brunettes and Farrah Fawcett (as Jill Munroe) was the blonde in the first season of Charlie's Angels. For the second season, Cheryl Ladd (as Kris Munroe) stepped in as the blonde, re- placing Farrah Fawcett. When Kate Jackson left in the fourth sea- son, blond Shelly Hack (as Tiffany Welles) joined the team. She lasted only one year and was replaced by a brunette, Tanya Roberts (as Julie Rogers).*

5. *Jack Tripper (John Ritter), Janet Wood (Joyce DeWitt), and Chrissy Snow (Suzanne Somers) were the original three roommates on Three's Company. Chrissy's cousin Cindy Snow (Jenilee Harri- son) moved in during the fifth season while Chrissy visited her sick mother. (Actually, Somers was being phased out of the series in the midst of a contract dispute.) In the sixth season, Cindy moved to her own apartment near her college and Terri Alden (Priscilla Barnes) replaced her as a roommate. Cindy still dropped by to visit occa- sionally. Helen and Stanley Roper (Audra Lindley and Norman Fell) collected the rent for the first three seasons, then Ralph Furley (Don Knotts) took over the apartment complex.*

6. *An abstract N. Soon after the new symbol was unveiled, a pub- lic-television station in Nebraska pointed out that the N was a dead ringer for its logo (designed at a fraction of the cost). Though NBC*

kept the N, the network also returned the peacock to active service within a few years.

7. *A house trailer on the beach.*

8. *Billie Jean King easily topped Bobby Riggs.*

9. *Gary Burghoff, as Corporal Walter "Radar" O'Reilly. He stayed with the series until 1979 (about 6½ seasons). Technically, another film performer, G. Wood, as General Hamilton Hammond, also came over to the TV version at the beginning of its run, but he quickly disappeared.*

10. *Steven Spielberg directed "Murder by the Book," the first entry in the regular* Columbo *series run as part of NBC's Wednesday Mystery Movie. This followed two successful made-for-TV pilot films (not directed by Spielberg) that had set up the Columbo character and basic series structure.*

11. All in the Family *was based on* Till Death Do Us Part; Sanford and Son *was based on* Steptoe and Son; *and* Three's Company *was based on* Man About the House.

12. *James Thurber.*

13. *On November 17, 1968, NBC cut from a Sunday afternoon football game still in progress in order to begin on time a heavily promoted new made-for-TV production of Heidi. It seemed a safe decision, with the New York Jets holding a comfortable lead over the Oakland Raiders and only one minute left to play. Unfortunately for NBC, while the special aired uninterrupted, East Coast viewers missed a stunning football comeback rally as Oakland scored twice to win the game.*

14. *Chief Robert Ironside (Raymond Burr) was wounded by a would-be assassin and left paralyzed from the waist down.*

15. *The mysterious one-armed man Richard Kimble had seen leaving the scene of the crime. Fred Johnson (Bill Raisch) confessed to Kimble in the final episode of* The Fugitive.

16. *Himself. William Dozier also did the narration for the companion* Green Hornet *TV series, but played down the camp hysterics on that one.*

17. *The passengers aboard the* Minnow *included: a millionaire (Jim Backus as Thurston Howell III) and his wife (Natalie Schafer as Lovey Howell III), a movie star (Tina Louise as Ginger Grant), a professor (Russell Johnson as Roy Hinkley), and a sweet country girl (Dawn Wells as Mary Ann Summers).*

18. *The Beatles. This was their first live performance on American television.*

19. The Jetsons, *Hanna-Barbera's mirror-image spin-off from* The Flintstones, *premiering in September 1962.*

20. *Richard M. Nixon (then vice president) was the Republican candidate and John F. Kennedy (then a U.S. senator) was the Democratic candidate.*

21. *Walter Cronkite.*

22. *Rod Serling, who opened and closed each episode.*

23. *Male. The final season of the series for CBS posed quite an acting challenge, because Lassie fell in love and had a litter of puppies.*

24. *Mike Wallace.*

25. *Howard Cosell.*

26. On The Mickey Mouse Club: *Monday was "Fun With Music Day"; Tuesday was "Guest Star Day"; Wednesday was "Anything Can Happen Day"; Thursday was "Circus Day"; and Friday was "Talent Roundup Day."*

27. *Davy Crockett, played by Fess Parker. Surprisingly, there were only five one-hour adventures of the character ever filmed, though they were all rerun several times.*

28. *J. Fred Muggs was a chimpanzee. He joined the show in early 1953 and no doubt helped the new program build its early-morning audience by giving children at home someone they could watch for.*

29. *That night the character of Lucy Ricardo gave birth to her first child. Earlier that same day, Lucille Ball had also given birth to a baby boy in real life. The perfect timing of the two births created a spectacular media event that practically overshadowed the inauguration of President Dwight Eisenhower the next day.*

30. *On his first* See It Now *broadcast, Edward R. Murrow sat before two television monitors in CBS's New York City Studio 41 and asked director Don Hewitt to punch up a live signal from the West Coast on one monitor while showing a scene from New York City on the other. Instantly both pictures appeared, side by side, giving Americans a view of both coasts of their vast continent at once, live and instantaneously.*

31. *Groucho Marx was quizmaster on NBC's* You Bet Your Life *while Chico Marx performed on ABC's* College Bowl, *a loose musical-comedy format set at a college campus soda shop.*

32. *Jennie Lewis, better known as Dagmar.*

33. *John Cameron Swayze.*

34. *Dean Martin and Jerry Lewis, demonstrating that, from the beginning, Ed Sullivan's eye for spotting up-and-coming talent was uncanny.*

35. *Milton Berle, nicknamed "Mr. Television."*

36. *"Big Brother" Bob Emery.*

37. Hour Glass, *which played on NBC from May 1946 to March 1947. This ground-breaking program's budget (including a then-extravagant $4,000 each week for talent) allowed for better sets and production values, putting it far ahead of virtually anything that preceded it on TV.*

38. The Gillette Cavalcade of Sports, *which helped to make professional boxing a television staple throughout the 1940s.*

39. *President Franklin D. Roosevelt.*

40. *Charles Francis Jenkins, who conducted the demonstration at his laboratory in downtown Washington.*

FIRST CHANNEL
Pioneers
Variety
The Forties in Review

Pioneers

Identify these broadcast pioneers:

1. Inventor of the wireless telegraphy system, the forerunner to radio and television.

2. Secretary of Commerce (later a U.S. president) who in 1927 became the first high-ranking government official to appear on television.

3. RCA executive whose determination to promote the development of TV earned him the title "Father of American Television."

4. Son of a Philadelphia cigar manufacturer who turned the CBS network into a money-making venture.

5. Stand-in (actually a small statue on a revolving platter) used by NBC's experimental station in the late 1920s because no human could endure the intense light.

6. The first scientist to develop a working all-electronic television system.

7. An innovative electronics manufacturer who set up his own television network in 1939 as a feisty challenger to CBS and NBC.

8. Radio news veteran who delivered the first commercial television newscast in 1941.

9. CBS newsman who set the standards for broadcast journalism with such programs as *See It Now*.

10. The "old redhead" who pioneered the "natural" style of talking directly to the broadcast audience.

11. The freckle-faced wooden puppet who became one of television's first kidvid superstars.

12. CBS producer responsible for such ground-breaking programs as *Toast of the Town, Studio One, Mr. I Magination,* and *The Goldbergs.*

13. Husband-and-wife talk show duo who came over from radio to NBC-TV in 1947 with such shows as *At Home, Ringside,* and *The Swift Home Service Club.*

14. The first black to host a network television series.

15. NBC programming chief responsible for the development of *Today, Tonight, Your Show of Shows,* and the big-budget special.

BACK IN A MINUTE

for the answers to "Pioneers"
But first . . .

Even though TV did not catch on as a national medium until the late 1940s, there were experimental television broadcasts back as far as the late 1920s. In the summer of 1929, just before the start of the Great Depression, there were twenty-two such television stations operating in the U.S.: eight in the New York City area; three in Chicago; two in Los Angeles; one each in Schenectady, Washington, D.C., and Pittsburgh; three in Massachusetts and one each in Florida, Oregon, and Iowa. Among the organizations running these stations were RCA, Westinghouse, General Electric, the Chicago Federation of Labor, and the University of Iowa.

ANSWERS

1. *Guglielmo Marconi.*

2. *Herbert Hoover.*

3. *(Gen.) David Sarnoff.*

4. *William Paley.*

5. *Felix the Cat.*

6. *Philo T. Farnsworth.*

7. *Allen B. DuMont.*

8. *Lowell Thomas.*

9. *Edward R. Murrow.*

10. *Arthur Godfrey.*

11. *Howdy Doody.*

12. *Worthington Miner.*

13. *John Reagan McCrary and Eugenia Lincoln Falkenburg, better known as Tex and Jinx.*

14. *Bob Howard.*

15. *Sylvester "Pat" Weaver.*

Variety

1. In early 1948, the Hooper organization conducted the first television ratings sweep of New York City. What variety program walked away with the number-one slot?

2. Perhaps the maddest moments in early live variety took place off camera, as the host of NBC's *Arrow Show* each week dashed from the TV studio to the Broadway stage for a performance of *High Button Shoes*. Who made this run?

3. What DuMont variety series served as a valuable TV training ground for such stars as Jerry Lester, Jackie Gleason, Jack Carter, and Larry Storch?

4. Milton Berle had a hammerlock on the Tuesday-night TV audience for years, even withstanding a challenge from God. Name that competing show and its host.

5. Max Liebman first brought together some of the principals for *Your Show of Shows* in 1949 as part of a Friday-night variety series. What was it called and which of the networks carried it?

6. The Chicago school of television emphasized innovation with a bare-bones budget, epitomized in 1949 by the casual variety of Dave Garroway and Studs Terkel. Name their shows.

7. The first series ever to play on all four networks lured viewers with an irresistible mixture of light variety and dance instruction. Name the show and its "hostess with the mostest."

8. In the late 1940s, Ed Sullivan provided the powerful

lead-in for another successful Sunday night variety show
for CBS. What big band leader was host of that program?

9. What four performers formed the solid acting ensemble of
Your Show of Shows, shining in parodies of such material
as *Shane, From Here to Eternity*, and *This is Your Life*?

10. Who was the first guest host on *Your Show of Shows*?

11. Who played Alice Kramden in the original Honeymooners sketches presented on DuMont's *Cavalcade of Stars*?

12. In the fall of 1950, NBC dazzled viewers with the *Colgate
Comedy Hour* and *Four Star Revue*, featuring different
headliners rotating the plum assignment of program host.
Yet after only a few months, one big-name radio personal-
ity left this rotation. Who was it?

13. Name the teen heartthrob who hosted NBC's early 1950s
musical series *Coke Time*.

14. One of ABC's first successful variety shows was the *TV
Teen Club*. Who was the host?

15. "Thanks for the Memories" was the theme song for what
popular NBC radio comic who came over to television in
the fall of 1950?

BACK IN A MINUTE

for the answers to "Variety"
But first . . .

Some Questions Even We Can't Answer:

Since Superman flew with his arms outstretched, how did he always come through the window feet first?

How did Lassie, Rin Tin Tin, and other animal heroes always manage to find humans who could understand their calls for help?

How many languages could Flipper speak?

Did Billy the Kid actually have the time for adventures with practically every TV Western hero?

Why did Charlie the Tuna *want* to be caught and canned?

ANSWERS

1. *Ted Mack's* Original Amateur Hour, *which registered a 46.8 rating—that is, of the television sets in the homes contacted, 46.8 percent were on and tuned to his program.*

2. *Phil Silvers. He soon called a halt to this madness and gave up the television show.*

3. Cavalcade of Stars, *which ran on DuMont from the summer of 1949 to the fall of 1952.*

4. *DuMont's* Life Is Worth Living, *hosted by Roman Catholic Bishop Fulton J. Sheen. When DuMont folded in 1955 the program went over to ABC, then into syndication during the 1960s as* The Bishop Sheen Program.

5. Admiral Broadway Revue, *which ran on both NBC and Du-Mont.*

6. *Dave Garroway hosted* Garroway at Large, *while Studs Terkel was head barkeep on Studs' Place.*

7. The Arthur Murray Party, *with Kathryn Murray as "the hostess with the mostest." The program ran from 1950 through 1960.*

8. *Fred Waring.*

9. *Sid Caesar, Imogene Coca, Carl Reiner, and Howard Morris were the performing backbone of* Your Show of Shows.

10. *Burgess Meredith hosted the first two programs in the series.*

11. *Pert Kelton. When Jackie Gleason moved to CBS in 1952, she was replaced in the role by Audrey Meadows.*

12. *Fred Allen, whose style of intimate radio humor was particularly ill suited to the flashy TV variety format imposed on him by*

NBC. Citing ill health, he left the hosting rotation in December 1950.

13. *Eddie Fisher.*

14. *Paul Whiteman.*

15. *Bob Hope.*

The Forties in Review

1. What happened to NBC's experimental station in New York City at 1:30 P.M. July 1, 1941?

2. In 1943, Edward J. Noble purchased the "Blue" network and, two years later, officially renamed it ABC. What company originally owned it?

3. On June 19, 1946, an estimated audience of 150,000 saw the first "television sports extravaganza," live in New York, Schenectady, Philadelphia, and Washington. What was it?

4. What was the format of the 1946 NBC series *I Love to Eat*?

5. How did stations not yet connected to the coaxial cable network manage to air live television shows?

6. What was the Petrillo ban?

7. Old Hopalong Cassidy films became a big hit with children during the late 1940s and early 1950s. Who owned the television rights to them?

8. One of NBC's earliest prime-time variety shows was the *Gulf Road Show* starring Bob Smith. What was Smith better known for?

9. In 1947, independent Jerry Fairbanks became the first Hollywood filmmaker to produce a filmed series specifically for television. Name the crime series that was the first show he filmed for that venture.

10. Name the longest-running network TV series still on the air, appearing on NBC from November 1947 to the present.

11. Who was the "guardian of the safety of the world" in one of DuMont's longest-running shows?

12. Name the 1948 comedy-variety show set at the "Golden Goose" nightclub, with Art Carney and Jacqueline Susann as supporting players.

13. What gimmick sport did ABC add to its schedule in 1949, showcasing such fierce competitors as Midge "Toughy" Brashun and Ann "Red" Jensen?

14. What was the original title for Allen Funt's *Candid Camera* series?

15. Though William Bendix originated the role of Chester A. Riley on radio, he did not play the character in the first television version in 1949. Who did?

ANSWERS

1. *NBC's New York City station made the changeover to commercial status, becoming WNBT. This marked the beginning of commercial television broadcasting in the United States.*

2. *NBC originally owned the "Blue" network system. In 1941, the FCC ordered NBC to divest itself of either its "Red" or "Blue" chain of stations. Following a series of unsuccessful appeals, NBC did so in 1943.*

3. *The heavyweight boxing championship fight between Joe Louis and Billy Conn. Louis won in eight rounds.*

4. I Love to Eat *was an appropriately named cooking instruction show.*

5. *Until 1947, local stations not yet connected to the coaxial cable network could not air live network television shows. Then DuMont unveiled a method of filming live programs directly from a television monitor. These kinescope recordings (dubbed "kines") were sent to any local stations that required them, providing copies of live shows that hit the air about a week or two after the original broadcast.*

6. *In February 1945, James C. Petrillo, president of the American Federation of Musicians, put a total ban on all television appearances by any of his union musicians. He did this to prevent any low-paying contract precedents from being set while union leaders and the networks worked out the pay scale for the new medium. The Petrillo ban lasted three years, effectively eliminating most music-related programming from the air. On March 20, 1948, the networks at last came to terms with Petrillo and signed lucrative new contracts.*

7. *A farsighted William Boyd, who played Hopalong Cassidy in* *the films. Early in the 1940s, he figured that his classic kiddie Westerns would be perfect for television, so he began buying up the TV rights. He was right on the money.*

8. *His role as "Buffalo" Bob Smith on Howdy Doody.*

9. Public Prosecutor. *Fairbanks filmed seventeen episodes of the series, each running twenty minutes. Jerry Fairbanks was a few years ahead of his time, however, and he found no buyers. The series remained on the shelf until the early 1950s.*

10. Meet the Press.

11. *Captain Video, played by Richard Coogan in 1949 and 1950, then by Al Hodge from 1951 to 1955.*

12. The Morey Amsterdam Show *on CBS.*

13. *Roller Derby.*

14. Candid Microphone, *which was the program's original title on ABC radio.*

15. *Jackie Gleason.*

STATION BREAK

Station Break

1. Experimental TV stations signed on in the United States as early as 1928. Match each station's call letters with its owner and location.

   W2XAB   CBS in New York
   W2XBS   Federation of Labor in Chicago
   W2XWV   DuMont in New York
   W2XCW   DuMont in Washington
   W3XWT   General Electric in Schenectady
   W9XAA   NBC in New York

2. The 1939 New York World's Fair gave many Americans their first chance to see television in action. What station broadcast from the grounds throughout the run of the fair?

3. Whatever happened to Channel 1?

4. Late-starting ABC began its television operations without a home base, using borrowed and temporary facilities until August 1948 when what station signed on?

5. By the summer of 1952, only one TV station in the entire country was not hooked in with the new coast-to-coast co-axial cable. What was it?

6. America's first commerical UHF station signed on October 1, 1952. What was it?

7. America's first noncommercial "educational" television station hit the air on May 25, 1953. What was it?

8. ABC, CBS, and NBC are each allowed five owned-and-

operated TV stations throughout the country. Name each network's current O&O cities.

9. What were DuMont's owned-and-operated stations and why did that network have only three?

10. In order to provide New York City with public television on the VHF band, a station was "brought in" from another state. Where was Channel 13 located?

ANSWERS

1. *W2XAB was CBS in New York; W2XBS was NBC in New York; W2XWV was DuMont in New York; W2XCW was General Electric in Schenectady; W3XWT was DuMont in Washington; and W9XAA was the Federation of Labor in Chicago.*

2. *W2XBS, which stationed a mobile van at the RCA Pavilion. There were also receivers set up at the exhibit so that people could see themselves on television.*

3. *On May 6, 1948, the FCC set aside the Channel 1 frequencies for use by the military. This took place before any station was ever allocated that position on the dial.*

4. *New York City's WJZ, later changed to WABC.*

5. *KOB in Albuquerque, New Mexico.*

6. *KPTV (Channel 27) in Portland, Oregon.*

7. *KUHT (Channel 8) in Houston, Texas.*

8. *ABC has O&O stations in New York (WABC), Chicago (WLS), Los Angeles (KABC), San Francisco (KGO), and Detroit (WXYZ). CBS has its O&O stations in New York (WCBS), Chicago (WBBM), Los Angeles (KNXT), St. Louis (KMOX), and Philadelphia (WCAU). NBC has its O&O stations in New York (WNBC), Chicago (WMAQ), Los Angeles (KNBC), Cleveland (WKYC), and Washington (WRC).*

9. *DuMont's O&O stations were in New York (WABD), Washington (WTTG), and Pittsburgh (WDTV). Because the FCC considered Paramount Pictures and DuMont to be part of the same corporate entity, the commission counted Paramount's two O&O stations (WBKB in Chicago and KTLA in Los Angeles) together with Du-Mont's, bringing the overall total to the limit of five.*

10. *Newark, New Jersey.*

SECOND CHANNEL
Kidvid
Sitcoms
Westerns
Game Shows
"Serious Drama"
The Fifties in Review

Kidvid

1. Who originally played the role of Clarabell the Clown on *Howdy Doody*?

2. What were "Danny Match," "Space Barton," "Johnny and Mr. Do-Right," and "Kid Champion"?

3. How did viewers participate directly in the adventures of Winky Dink?

4. One of the few cartoon features to be regularly included on *Captain Kangaroo* was "Tom Terrific." What gave the pint-size hero the power to turn into practically anything? Who was his ever faithful companion? Who was his rotten-to-the-core nemesis?

5. What city was the original broadcast home for *Super Circus, Mr. Wizard, Ding Dong School,* and *Kukla, Fran and Ollie*?

6. In 1955, CBS brought the first animated cartoon series to Saturday-morning network TV. What was the title character of the show?

7. In the opening sequence to *The Mickey Mouse Club*, Donald Duck was consistently frustrated in his attempts to strike a gong. Did he ever do so successfully?

8. What was Hanna-Barbera's first made-for-TV cartoon series for network television?

9. What character from *The Huckleberry Hound Show* was Hanna-Barbera's most popular by far, spinning off into his own TV series and a feature-length movie?

10. What kidvid series featured such popular nonhumans as Bullet, Buttercup, and Nelliebelle?

11. What was the connection between the Lone Ranger and the Green Hornet?

12. From 1952 to 1954, who replaced Clayton Moore in the title role of *The Lone Ranger*?

13. In the television treatment of Superman, who played: The Man of Steel? Lois Lane? Jor-el on Krypton?

14. Who was the narrator for the cliff-hanger adventures of Rocky and Bullwinkle?

15. Was there ever a Rocky and Bullwinkle serial that did *not* include Boris and Natasha?

16. Historical anachronisms in the "Peabody's Improbable History" segment of *The Bullwinkle Show* were actually explained in the very first episode. How did they occur?

17. What was the original name of the Jetson family's pet dog?

18. Members of Captain Midnight's Secret Squadron had to blink twice when the CBS series went into rerun syndication, because there was a new title and some new dialogue dubbed over the old stories. What was the hero's new name and why was it changed?

19. What was the gimmick of Mr. Magoo's prime-time series for NBC?

20. In the fall of 1964, CBS replaced its Saturday-morning *Captain Kangaroo* reruns with a new children's series, *Mister Mayor.* Who played the mayor?

ANSWERS

1. *Bob Keeshan, later known as Captain Kangaroo.*

2. *All four were three-minute animated series that made up NBC Comics, a fifteen-minute late-afternoon weekday cartoon program that premiered on September 18, 1950. It was the first animated cartoon series on network television. The respective hooks were: a young private eye ("Danny Match"); interplanetary adventures ("Space Barton"); a schoolboy and his dog ("Johnny and Mr. Do-Right"); and a young boxer ("Kid Champion").*

3. *After purchasing a special plastic sheet to place on their home TV screens, viewers could help Winky Dink out of predicaments by drawing in such items as a bridge over a chasm. Of course, some kids did not bother with the plastic sheet and drew directly onto the TV screen. Others did not draw at all, but had to puzzle out just how Winky Dink managed to escape without their help.*

4. *Tom Terrific's magic thinking cap, which looked suspiciously like a kitchen funnel, allowed him to change into anything. Mighty Manfred, the wonder dog, was his ever faithful companion, while the fiendish Crabby Appleton was his rotten-to-the-core nemesis.*

5. *Chicago.*

6. *Mighty Mouse. These were not original made-for-TV cartoons, however, but repackagings of Terrytoons material that had first played as theatrical shorts.*

7. *Yes. And even he looked astounded at the accomplishment.*

8. *Ruff and Reddy, the cliff-hanger adventures of Ruff the cat and his friend Reddy, a tall dog with a southern accent.*

9. *Yogi Bear. The 1964 feature film was called "Hey There, It's Yogi Bear."*

10. The Roy Rogers Show, *featuring Roy Rogers and Dale Evans playing themselves. Bullet was Roy's pet German shepherd, Buttercup was Dale's horse, and Nelliebelle was the name of the jeep driven by sidekick Pat Brady.*

11. *George Trendle and Fran Striker, who created and wrote both series on radio, tied the characters' lives together by making John (the Lone Ranger) Reid's nephew, Dan, the father of Britt Reid (the Green Hornet).*

12. *John Hart.*

13. *George Reeves played the dual role of Superman and his Clark Kent alter ego. Phyllis Coates played Lois Lane in the first twenty-six episodes; Noel Neill took over thereafter. Robert Rockwell (better known as Philip Boynton on Our Miss Brooks) appeared as Jor-el on Krypton in the episode about Superman's origin.*

14. *William Conrad.*

15. *Yes, most notably the story that featured Bullwinkle as a master swordsman (due to his skill at skewering shish kebab). In the comic-book series published at the time, Boris even alluded to that TV adventure by complaining, "That's one they left us out of!"*

16. *At first, Peabody had built a straightforward time machine (the Way-Back) but discovered that he and Sherman could not participate in the events they visited. So he modified the device, changing it into a "should-have-been" machine that stretched and altered reality, allowing them to have their own adventures with characters in the past.*

17. *"Tralfaz Gotrockets," after his previous master, Mr. Gotrockets. When the Jetson family took the dog in, his name became the much more concise "Astro."*

18. *Jet Jackson, the Flying Commando. The name was changed because Ovaltine, which owned the rights to the name "Captain Midnight" from back in its original radio run, did not come along as the sponsor for the syndicated TV rerun package. Besides changing the title graphic, the producers also removed all references to "Captain Midnight" in the dialogue, overdubbing the new name when necessary.*

19. *No doubt inspired by the success of an animated TV special of* A Christmas Carol, *which cast Mr. Magoo as Scrooge, The Famous Adventures of Mr. Magoo placed the character in different settings from history and literature. He became a sort of one-man repertory company.*

20. *Bob Keeshan.*

Sitcoms

1. Like its radio counterpart, TV's *Amos and Andy* focused primarily on the adventures of what nontitle character?

2. In one episode of *I Love Lucy*, Lucy and guest Harpo Marx did a tribute restaging of what famous scene from the Marx Brothers movie *Duck Soup*?

3. How did the titles *You'll Never Get Rich*, *Make Room for Daddy*, *Where's Raymond?*, and *I Love Lucy* tie in to their respective series?

4. What series featured tales of a wacky wife as told by her husband (a judge) in his courtroom?

5. Where was Jack Benny's home safe located?

6. What did the character of Jack Benny do for a living?

7. What friend of George Burns made a number of cameo appearances on *The Burns and Allen Show*, once acting as "bottom man" for a human pyramid?

8. On *My Little Margie*, who was Margie Albright's father and who did he work for?

9. Jim Anderson was a suburban TV father who actually did have a job. What did he do for a living on *Father Knows Best*?

10. Who was host to a pair of ghosts (and their dog)?

11. What line did Bob Cummings use each week to open his sitcom series about a girl-crazy photographer?

12. Name Jefferson High School's shy science teacher, brash

history teacher, befuddled English teacher, and kind but quiet school nurse.

13. Name Madison High School's blustery principal, shy biology teacher, sharp-tongued English teacher, and quintessential squeaky-voiced problem student.

14. Andy of Mayberry, Jose the elevator operator, and producer Sheldon Leonard all popped up on what popular family sitcom?

15. One off-camera character on *December Bride* was never seen in that series but still won a spin-off show. Name the character and the other series.

16. Who put words in the mouths of Cleo, the basset hound on *The People's Choice*, and Mr. Ed, the golden palomino?

17. What was unusual about Charley, Enoch, and Candy, the children in *The Hathaways*?

18. In what hit sitcom of the late 1950s did Warren Beatty play the part of a handsome athletic teen?

19. Which was which in *I'm Dickens, He's Fenster*?

20. Near what statue did Dobie Gillis frequently deliver his asides to the audience?

ANSWERS

1. *George Stevens (Tim Moore), better known as "the Kingfish."*

2. *The "missing mirror" scene in which Harpo (disguised as Groucho) stood facing the real Groucho in a doorway that had previously contained a full-length mirror and tried to convince him that the mirror was still there by matching his every move. Amazingly, in this scene Lucille Ball and Harpo Marx passed for look-alikes as well.*

3. You'll Never Get Rich. *The title came from a line in the song "You're in the Army Now," a direct reference to the setting of the sitcom: an American army base. Nonetheless, the series was soon renamed* The Phil Silvers Show, *though most people referred to it as* Sgt. Bilko.

Make Room for Daddy. *Danny Thomas played a nightclub performer who was frequently on the road. When he came back home, his children had to shift their quarters around to "make room for daddy." Thomas changed the title to* The Danny Thomas Show, *but the original was used for the syndicated rerun package.*

Where's Raymond? *Ray Bolger played a professional song-and-dance man who usually arrived at the theater only minutes before he was to step on stage. As a result, the crew constantly wondered, "Where's Raymond?"*

I Love Lucy. *CBS wanted to call the program something like* The Lucille Ball Show. *Lucy wanted Desi in the title. They compromised with* I Love Lucy, *because the "I" referred to Desi's character.*

4. I Married Joan. *Jim Backus played Judge Bradley Stevens and Joan Davis played his wacky wife.*

5. *In an underground vault hidden beneath his home and protected by elaborate booby traps and a dedicated Civil War soldier.*

6. *He was host of a television comedy-variety show. This show-*

within-a-show premise allowed the actual Jack Benny Program *to alternate easily between a standard comedy-variety setting some weeks and sitcom type off-camera complications during others.*

7. *Jack Benny.*

8. *Charles Farrell played Vernon Albright, who worked for George Honeywell (Clarence Kolb) at the investment firm of Honeywell and Todd.*

9. *Jim Anderson sold insurance for the General Insurance Company.*

10. *Leo G. Carroll in the title role of Cosmo Topper.*

11. The Bob Cummings Show, *called* Love That Bob *in syndication, opened with the line: "Hold it! I think you're gonna like this picture."*

12. *Jefferson High School was the setting for NBC's* Mr. Peepers, *which featured: Wally Cox as Robinson Peepers, a shy science teacher; Tony Randall as Harvey Weskit, a brash history teacher; Marion Lorne as Mrs. Gurney, a befuddled English teacher; and Patricia Benoit as Nancy Remington, the school nurse.*

13. *Madison High School was the setting for CBS's* Our Miss Brooks, *which featured: Gale Gordon as Osgood Conklin, the principal; Robert Rockwell as Philip Boynton, the shy biology teacher; Eve Arden as Connie Brooks, the sharp-tongued English teacher; and Richard Crenna as Walter Denton, the squeaky-voiced problem student.*

14. The Danny Thomas Show. *Bill Dana's character of Jose Jiminez and Andy Griffith's character of a small-town sheriff were both placed in their own series after pilot appearances on Thomas's show. Program producer Sheldon Leonard appeared in a number of roles over the years, including stints as Danny's agent and personal masseur.*

15. *Gladys Porter (Cara Williams), whose off-camera antics had been described for years by her husband Pete (Harry Morgan) on* December Bride, *shared co-billing on the 1960 spin-off,* Pete and Gladys.

16. *Mary Jane Croft supplied the voice for Cleo on* The People's

Choice, *while Allan "Rocky" Lane did the same for Mr. Ed.*

17. *They were chimpanzees, played by the Marquis Chimps (a popular animal act of the early 1960s).*

18. On The Many Loves of Dobie Gillis, *Warren Beatty played Milton Armitage, Dobie's rival for the affections of Thalia Menninger.*

19. *John Astin played Harry Dickens and Marty Ingels played Arch Fenster.*

20. The Thinker, *often assuming the pose himself.*

Westerns

1. In the 1955 opening episode of *Gunsmoke*, what sage-brush veteran introduced viewers to the series?

2. What three feature-film leads cut their teeth on the Western adventures of (respectively) *Wanted: Dead or Alive*, *Rawhide*, and *Riverboat*?

3. What Western began as a segment in the 1955 *Warner Brothers Presents* program that presented TV series adaptations of several films from the studio's archives?

4. What was unusual about the births of Hoss, Adam, and Little Joe in the epic family drama of *Bonanza*?

5. Over the years the Maverick kin included: three brothers, their dad, his brother, a British cousin, and his son. Name them.

6. What was printed on Paladin's calling card?

7. What was so unusual about the production setup for CBS's daytime Western *Action in the Afternoon*?

8. What popular game show emcee of the 1960s was previously a co-star of NBC's Western series *The Californians*?

9. What series had as its theme song "The Ballad of Johnny Yuma," sung by Country-and-Western star Johnny Cash?

10. How did the title character of *Sugarfoot* get his nickname?

11. Who was the dedicated town marshal (and series narrator) in *The Deputy*?

12. What series emphasized the warm interaction between a hardworking rancher and his young son?

13. What reluctant Western hero spent his spare time taking a correspondence course to become a lawyer?

14. What Western dandy used a cane and a derby hat as his gimmick calling cards?

15. What made rancher Sky King's adventures different from other kidvid Westerns?

16. What former "rifle-toting" cowboy played the lone survivor of "the battle of Bitter Creek" and what was the series?

17. Who was the wagon master for the yearly trip west to California from St. Joseph, Missouri?

18. What NBC Western provided an unexpected boost to color TV set sales in the late 1950s with its wide expanses of full-color scenery?

19. Who was The Virginian?

20. Nearly a decade after playing Davy Crockett on ABC, Fess Parker turned up as another frontiersman-scout for NBC. Name that series.

BACK IN A MINUTE

for the answers to "Westerns"
But first . . .

Very often in the history of television one particular format catches on with the public, and network programmers respond by overloading prime time with similar fare. The flood of TV Westerns in the late 1950s signalled the high-water mark of this programming copycat syndrome. By the fall of 1959, network TV viewers had their choice from a staggering twenty-eight different Western-based prime time series: two on Wednesdays, three on Mondays, four on both Thursdays and Fridays, and five each on Sundays, Tuesdays, and Saturdays.

ANSWERS

1. *John Wayne, who had suggested James Arness for the lead.*

2. *Steve McQueen (as Josh Randall) on* Wanted: Dead or Alive; *Clint Eastwood (as Rowdy Yates) on* Rawhide; *and Burt Reynolds (as Ben Frazer) on* Riverboat.

3. Cheyenne. *It was the only segment of* Warner Brothers Presents *that survived the first season and caught on.*

4. *Ben Cartwright had been married three times, and each of his wives had given birth to one of the sons.*

5. *The* Maverick *kin consisted of: brothers Bret (James Garner), Bart (Jack Kelly), and Brent (Robert Colbert); their pappy, Beauregard (James Garner); their dad's brother, "Uncle" Bentley (Jack Kelly); their polished-in-Britain cousin, Beauregard (Roger Moore); and Beau's son, Ben (Charles Frank).*

6. *"Have Gun, Will Travel . . . Wire Paladin, San Francisco."*

7. *The program was done live from an outdoor studio lot in Philadelphia.*

8. *Art Fleming played Jeremy Pitt in* The Californians *but was later best known as the emcee of NBC's* Jeopardy.

9. *ABC's* The Rebel, *starring Nick Adams as Johnny Yuma.*

10. *In the series plot line, Tom Brewster (Will Hutchins) was set up to be so inept and inexperienced as a cowboy that even the term "tenderfoot" seemed too good for him. He was worse: a "sugarfoot."*

11. *Henry Fonda.*

12. The Rifleman, *featuring Chuck Connors as the dad and Johnny Crawford as his son.*

13. *Tom Brewster, the Sugarfoot. (No wonder he was such a poor cowboy!)*

14. *Bat Masterson (Gene Barry).*

15. *Sky King (Kirby Grant) was a former World War II aviator who fought the bad guys from his small plane,* The Songbird, *instead of riding a horse.*

16. *Former* Rifleman *star Chuck Connors in* Branded.

17. *For the first five years of* Wagon Train, *Ward Bond played the wagon master, Major Seth Adams. John McIntire (as Chris Hale) took over the task when Bond died, staying on for the duration of the series.*

18. Bonanza.

19. *James Drury played the title role in* The Virginian, *though the mysterious character's real name was never revealed in the nine-year run of the series.*

20. Daniel Boone.

BAYVIEW MIDDLE SCHOOL LIBRARY

Game Shows

1. What popular parlor game became one of the most frequently used hooks for early TV game shows such as *Stump the Stars?*

2. Who was the energetic master of ceremonies on *Stop the Music, County Fair, Bid'n'Buy,* and *Double or Nothing?*

3. One of the writers for the flashy *$64,000 Question* was a university professor who also hosted his own quiz program—a witty panel show that eventually played on all four networks. Name the host and his series.

4. Dr. Joyce Brothers won *The $64,000 Question* in her chosen category, boxing, by correctly describing a cestus. What is it?

5. In *The Honeymooners* parody of the big-money giveaway shows, Ralph Kramden mastered the subject of music but blanked out on the first question. What tune did he fail to identify?

6. Name the Marine Corps major (and future senator) who won $15,000 on *Name That Tune* in the mid-1950s, correctly identifying such songs as "Far Away Places."

7. The following were among the questions put to big-money winner Charles Van Doren on *Twenty-One.* He missed one. Can you outscore him?
   a) Name the Polish volunteer who became Washington's aide in the Revolutionary War.
   b) Define "caries."
   c) Name the city and the church that houses Leonardo da Vinci's "Last Supper" fresco.
   d) Name the king of Belgium (in 1957).

8. What pair of producers were responsible for *Tic Tac Dough, Twenty-One,* and *The Joker's Wild*?

9. Who were the two producers of such hit game shows as *I've Got a Secret, What's My Line, To Tell the Truth, The Match Game,* and *Family Feud*?

10. Name the ABC daytime game show of the late 1950s, hosted by Dick Van Dyke, that placed mothers in competition doing household chores.

11. Teddy Nadler was the top TV game show money winner of the 1950s. How much did he win and on what show?

12. What game show offered as its grand prize a total of $1.98 in cash?

13. The 1950s quiz show scandal actually developed out of a complaint lodged against the daytime version of a relatively obscure quizzer. Name that show.

14. Name the 1960 quizzer that lasted one week before host Jackie Gleason scrapped that format and turned the show into a loose comedy-variety program.

15. What popular daytime game show hosted by Jack Bailey used an on-screen audience applause meter to determine each day's winner?

16. What was the twist contestants faced in playing *Jeopardy?*

17. Who was the original host of *Video Village*?

18. Name the syndicated game show that then-governor Jimmy Carter appeared on in 1973.

19. Who was the original host of *Do You Trust Your Wife?*

20. Who hosted NBC's 1981 world-hopping winner-take-all marathon contest, "The All-American Ultra Quiz"?

ANSWERS

1. *Charades.*

2. *Bert Parks.*

3. *Dr. Bergen Evans hosted* Down You Go.

4. *Joyce Brothers identified "cestus" as the special gloves worn by gladiators in ancient Rome.*

5. *Stephen Foster's "Swanee River," which Ed Norton had played as a warm-up at the piano throughout the episode.*

6. *John Glenn.*

7. *a) Tadeusz Kosciuszko was Washington's aide;*
   b) "Caries" is another name for dental cavities;
   c) "The Last Supper" is in Milan at the Santa Maria delle Grázie church.
   d) The king of Belgium was named Baudouin.
   Charles Van Doren missed the last question in his final appearance on Twenty-One.

8. *Jack Barry and Dan Enright.*

9. *Mark Goodson and Bill Todman.*

10. Mother's Day.

11. *Teddy Nadler won a quarter of a million dollars ($252,000 to be exact) on* The $64,000 Challenge.

12. *Chuck Barris's syndicated* $1.98 Beauty Contest.

13. Dotto *on* CBS, *but the investigation soon led to other shows.*

14. You're in the Picture.

15. Queen for a Day.

16. *Contestants had to provide appropriate questions to fit answers that they were given in particular categories.*

17. *Jack Narz. He was succeeded by Monty Hall.*

18. What's My Line.

19. *Edgar Bergen, who stayed with the program through its prime-time run (1956–1957). Johnny Carson took over when the show moved to daytime in the fall of 1957, when the title was eventually changed to* Who Do You Trust?*.*

20. *Dan Rowan and Dick Martin.*

"Serious Drama"

1. What was the first television drama series with a regular sponsor, beginning its run on May 7, 1947?

2. *Studio One's* 1949 staging of *Julius Caesar* used an effective costuming device to make the Shakespearean play especially relevant to the TV audience. What was it?

3. The story of a hardworking unmarried butcher who found companionship with an equally lonely young woman was hailed as a milestone in the golden age of TV drama. Name the story, the writer, and the lead.

4. In *Twelve Angry Men,* Robert Cummings played the lone juror voting "not guilty" in a murder case. As the play unfolded, he attempted to convince the eleven others to join him. What was the final jury vote?

5. *Gomer Pyle, U.S.M.C.* was essentially the same format as a 1955 play on *The U.S. Steel Hour* featuring Andy Griffith as a farm boy drafted into the Air Force. Name the play.

6. In the spring of 1953, what two CBS comedy-variety stars appeared in *The Laugh Maker,* a serious drama presentation on *Studio One?*

7. What story of the high-pressure world of big business starring Richard Kiley, Everett Sloan, and Ed Begley provided the big break for writer Rod Serling?

8. In *Studio One's Incredible World of Horace Ford,* Art Carney played a toy maker who longed to return to his childhood—and did. This same story was later restaged on what filmed fantasy series?

9. In 1956, Paul Newman starred as the main character–narrator in a tragic sports story on CBS's *U.S. Steel Hour.* Name the play.

10. Give the title and author of the satirical fantasy of a super-powered visitor to Earth, Mr. Kreton (played by Cyril Ritchard).

11. What song did Frank Sinatra popularize in a 1955 adaptation of Thornton Wilder's *Our Town* on NBC's *Producer's Showcase?*

12. In *The DuPont Show of the Month's Harvey* (with Art Carney), what was so unusual about the character of Harvey?

13. What mid-1960s sitcom star had previously appeared on her father's NBC drama anthology series of the 1950s?

14. What real-life father and son both had key roles in *Playhouse 90's Requiem for a Heavyweight?*

15. Who were the two leads in the 1958 television production of *The Days of Wine and Roses?*

16. What network broadcast an hour-long live drama from Los Angeles every weekday afternoon from late 1955 through 1958?

17. John Cameron Swayze, Douglas Edwards, and Ron Cochran each served as host–narrator of the *Armstrong Circle Theater.* What other on-camera job did they have in common, albeit on different networks?

18. Name the 1964 series of historical dramatizations inspired by John Kennedy's Pulitzer Prize-winning book.

19. Humphrey Bogart's only television drama appearance recreated one of his first hit roles, gangster Duke Mantee. What was the play?

20. What popular early 1960s drama series was based on a two-part story (starring Ralph Bellamy and William Shatner) presented in 1957 on *Studio One?*

ANSWERS

1. The Kraft Television Theater on *NBC*.

2. *The performers wore contemporary clothing rather than Roman robes. This made the story much more accessible and also underscored the timeless themes of totalitarian oppression and political conspiracy.*

3. Marty, *written by Paddy Chayefsky and starring Rod Steiger in the title role.*

4. *All twelve voted "not guilty."*

5. No Time for Sergeants.

6. *Jackie Gleason and Art Carney.*

7. Patterns. *The play received such acclaim after its presentation on NBC's* Kraft Television Theater *that it was restaged less than a month later. Serling also did the script for the subsequent feature-film version.*

8. The Twilight Zone, *during the program's fourth season when each episode played for a full hour.*

9. Bang the Drum Slowly.

10. Visit to a Small Planet, *written by Gore Vidal.*

11. *"Love and Marriage."*

12. *Harvey was a six-foot-tall invisible rabbit.*

13. *Elizabeth Montgomery (of Bewitched), appearing on her dad's program* Robert Montgomery Presents.

14. *Ed Wynn played the trainer to Jack Palance's character of a washed-up, dumb, but honest boxer. Wynn's son Keenan played the boxer's manager.*

15. *Piper Laurie and Cliff Robertson.*

16. *NBC. The network frequently aired episodes of* The NBC Matinee Theater *in color as part of its continuing effort to promote color set sales.*

17. *Each man also served as anchor for the evening news. John Cameron Swayze was on NBC, Douglas Edwards was on CBS, and Ron Cochran was on ABC.*

18. Profiles in Courage.

19. The Petrified Forest, *performed on NBC's* Producer's Showcase *in May 1955.*

20. The Defenders.

The Fifties in Review

1. What series featured the network television debut of Elvis Presley?

2. What was the Beaver's real name?

3. Who was Checkers in Richard Nixon's 1952 television address dubbed "The Checkers Speech"?

4. What did Arthur Godfrey say that his young protégé, Julius La Rosa, lacked when he explained why he had fired the singer?

5. Who was Jack Webb's TV partner during the last six years of *Dragnet*'s run in the 1950s—and who took over seven years later in the revival?

6. *My Favorite Husband* came to television in 1953 without its original radio lead. Who had played Liz Cooper on radio and who assumed the role for the TV version?

7. What was Edward R. Murrow's prime-time celebrity interview program, which visited the homes of such people as Harpo Marx and John Kennedy?

8. *The Ford 50th Anniversary Show* in 1953 scored tremendously high ratings. What advantage did it have over most other specials?

9. On March 7, 1955, NBC's *Producer's Showcase* presented what was then the highest-rated show of television's young history. What magical special production entranced nearly half the country that night?

10. Why did Sunday afternoon in the 1950s become known as "egghead" time?

11. David Janssen's first important TV series also featured Mary Tyler Moore's legs. Name the program.

12. The first television version of the Hardy Boys appeared as segments serialized on what popular 1950s children's show?

13. *American Bandstand* started as a local program hosted by disc jockey Bob Horn. Where did it originate?

14. Who was the substitute host of Ed Sullivan's show the first time Elvis Presley appeared as a guest?

15. What was the connection between John Beresford Tipton and Michael Anthony?

16. In the late 1950s, what local TV station pioneered: placing Bugs Bunny in prime time; slicing old jungle adventure films into a weekly series; and packaging old movies into a successful prime-time feature slot?

17. Who were the four stars of CBS's 1952 program *Four Star Playhouse*?

18. Why did *Father Knows Best* end production in 1959 even though it was still a top-ten show?

19. Though DuMont ceased to function as a major network in the mid-1950s, it continued to operate a chain of owned-and-operated TV stations under a different name. What was DuMont's new corporate identity?

20. Who did the voice-over narration for *The Untouchables*?

ANSWERS

1. CBS's *Stage Show, starring Tommy and Jimmy Dorsey. Elvis Presley first appeared on the program on January 28, 1956, singing "Blue Suede Shoes" and "Heartbreak Hotel." He returned to the show five more times that season.*

2. *Theodore Cleaver, played by Jerry Mathers.*

3. *Checkers was the name of a little black-and-white spotted cocker spaniel dog that Richard Nixon claimed a supporter from Texas had sent to the family. Because Nixon successfully emphasized such heart-tugging items in what might have been just a dry denial of some campaign "slush fund" charges, this address was nicknamed the Checkers speech.*

4. *Humility. Apparently Julius La Rosa had violated one of the unwritten rules of Arthur Godfrey's program cast by hiring his own agent and negotiating his own independent recording contract outside the show.*

5. *Ben Alexander played Officer Frank Smith from 1953 to 1959. Harry Morgan took over the job in the 1967 revival, playing Officer Bill Gannon.*

6. *Lucille Ball had played the lead in* My Favorite Husband *on radio. Joan Caulfield assumed the role for the TV version until 1955, when Vanessa Brown took over.*

7. Person to Person.

8. *The sponsor decided to purchase time on all the networks, so the program played on ABC, CBS, DuMont, and NBC at the same time. There was no network competition.*

9. Peter Pan.

10. *The networks regarded the time period as expendable and*

*placed many of their public-affairs and high-class cultural pro-
grams there, freeing the more valuable slots (especially prime time)
for mass-appeal entertainment shows. As a result, Sunday afternoon
took on a very serious ("egghead") tone. During the winter of 1955,
for instance, the following shows ran on NBC between 1:00 P.M. and
5:30 P.M.:* Princeton '65, Frontiers of Faith, American Inventory,
NBC Television Opera Theater, Juvenile Jury, Zoo Parade, *and*
Hallmark Hall of Fame.

11. Richard Diamond, Private Detective. *David Janssen had the
title role while Mary Tyler Moore played "Sam," the operator at his
answering service who was shown only from the waist down.*

12. The Mickey Mouse Club. *Tim Considine and Tommy Kirk
played the Hardy Boys in two serialized stories,* The Mystery of the
Applegate Treasure *and* The Mystery of Ghost Farm.

13. *Philadelphia.*

14. *Charles Laughton.*

15. *John Beresford Tipton was the multimillion-dollar eccentric
who each week on CBS's* The Millionaire *had his personal secretary, Michael Anthony (Marvin Miller) deliver a check for one million dollars to some unsuspecting soul.*

16. *WGN in Chicago. A creative young programmer named Fred
Silverman worked there at the time but soon moved on to CBS in
New York City.*

17. *The co-owners of Four Star Productions: Charles Boyer, Ida
Lupino, David Niven, and Dick Powell.*

18. *Robert Young, who had played the lead role of Jim Anderson
for eleven years—including five on radio preceding the TV series—
decided he wanted to move on, so the series was canceled. Prime-
time reruns continued, however, first on CBS and then on ABC, until 1963.*

19. *Metromedia.*

20. *Walter Winchell.*

COMMERCIAL BREAK

Commercial Break

1. Describe the first television commercial, aired July 1, 1941.

2. In 1947, Kraft staged the first major television ad campaign. Name the show, the product, and the results.

3. Name the oil company that sponsored Milton Berle's first television series.

4. NBC's 1950 *Your Show of Shows* instituted a new way for advertisers to buy into a show: participating sponsorship. What was it?

5. What 1950s game show had contestants bid for prizes using labels from Libby food products rather than money?

6. Match the product with one of its identifying commercial lines:

Ajax laundry detergent	"A breed apart."
Anacin	"Mother, please. I'd rather do it myself!"
Merrill Lynch investments	"Sorry, Charlie."
Pepsodent toothpaste	"Stronger than dirt!"
Star Kist tuna	"You'll wonder where the yellow went."

7. What large producer of household appliances featured Betty Furness in its commercials during the 1950s?

8. What brand of coffee was touted over the years by Ger-

trude Berg on *The Goldbergs,* Andy Griffith on *The Andy Griffith Show,* and Robert Young in commercial vignettes?

9. Name "the only cereal in the storybook package."

10. As if to prove that the prime-time *Flintstones* cartoon series was indeed aimed at adults, one of its sponsors in the first season was what cigarette company?

11. What product's award-winning campaign had as its theme "No Matter What Shape Your Stomach's In"?

12. Prior to her role on *Get Smart,* Barbara Feldon purred the praises of what product from a seductive position on a leopard skin?

13. Satirist Stan Freberg made fun of the mid-1960s "show us your Lark pack" cigarette ad campaign in a late 1960s ad for what food producer?

14. Match the product with one of its celebrity touts:

Edie Adams	Axion laundry detergent
Arthur Godfrey	Chrysler cars
Frank Sinatra	Muriel cigars
John Cameron Swayze	Timex watches
Don Wilson	Western Union Candygrams

15. At the same time that "I'd Like to Teach the World to Sing" was a top-ten hit for the New Seekers, it was also the commercial jingle for what product?

16. What was the first comic-book character to have a TV ad campaign devoted just to selling the comic magazine?

17. On January 1, 1971, a federal law took effect that banned radio and TV advertising for what product?

18. At the same time she was acting as maid to the McMillans and mother to Rhoda, Nancy Walker was also pushing what product in the commercial world?

19. Match the product with one of its cartoon character touts:

Bugs Bunny   Ford cars
Mr. Magoo   General Electric light bulbs
A pair of Muppets   Kellogg's Sugar Frosted
          Flakes
The Peanuts gang   Kool Aid
Tony the Tiger   Kramel Milk

20. What successful ad campaign resulted in Mariette Hartley being mistakenly identified as James Garner's wife?

ANSWERS

1. *Bulova sponsored a time, temperature, and weather check on NBC that included a Bulova watch ticking on screen for sixty seconds.*

2. The Kraft Television Theater *devoted all of the commercial time during its first two broadcasts of May 1947 to extolling Kraft's Mc-Laren's Imperial Cheese, a slow-selling new product with a then-extravagant price of one dollar per pound. Within two weeks, every package available in the New York City area had been sold.*

3. *Texaco.*

4. *Participating sponsorship allowed an individual sponsor to purchase one or two commercial spots on a program. Other sponsors could also do the same. Previously, the emphasis had been on one sponsor providing complete commercial support for an entire show, as in* The Texaco Star Theater. *Participating sponsorship opened television advertising to sponsors who were unable to carry an entire show, while also allowing the networks to charge more for each individual spot.*

5. Auction-Aire.

6. *Ajax laundry detergent was touted by a knight on a white charger as "stronger than dirt."*

Anacin offered relief to a harried housewife who was so tense and irritable that she snapped at her mother's offer of help in the kitchen with the line, "Mother, please. I'd rather do it myself."

Merrill Lynch investments, with a powerful bull as its symbol, declared that it was "a breed apart."

Pepsodent toothpaste promised to be so effective at cleaning teeth that customers were assured, "You'll wonder where the yellow went."

Star Kist tuna demonstrated its selective approach to tuna by re-

fusing the pleas of Charlie, a status-seeking fish that wanted to be caught and canned. A note on the Star Kist hook read: "Sorry, Charlie."

7. Westinghouse.

8. Sanka.

9. Twinkles. The story began on the front of the package, continued on the side panel, and concluded on the back. Twinkles was a magical pink elephant.

10. Winston cigarettes.

11. Alka-Seltzer. The T-Bones had a hit record with the instrumental tune in 1966, reaching the top five.

12. Top Brass hair care for men.

13. Jeno's Pizza. The ad was for Jeno's Pizza Rolls and featured the music used by the Lark company, Rossini's "William Tell Overture." This was also the theme music used on The Lone Ranger, so both Tonto and the Ranger appeared in the Jeno's commercial as well.

14. Edie Adams touted Muriel cigars;
Arthur Godfrey touted Axion laundry detergent;
Frank Sinatra touted Chrysler cars;
John Cameron Swayze touted Timex watches; and
Don Wilson touted Western Union Candygrams.

15. Coca-Cola.

16. Marvel's GI Joe in 1982. Though comic-book characters had appeared in television commercials for years, usually touting toys, this was the first time the comic book itself was the subject of the commercial campaign.

17. Cigarettes.

18. Bounty paper towels.

19. Bugs Bunny touted Kool Aid;
Mr. Magoo touted General Electric light bulbs;
A pair of Muppets touted Kramel Milk;
The Peanuts gang touted Ford cars; and
Tony the Tiger touted Kellogg's Sugar Frosted Flakes.

20. *A campaign for Polaroid cameras and film. The two performers were set in a series of humorous vignettes and seemed so natural together that people began to assume they were married. They weren't, though early in the ad campaign Mariette Hartley did turn up at Jim Rockford's door for an episode of James Garner's NBC series, The Rockford Files. Polaroid eventually mixed in a few spots with Garner or Hartley alone or even teamed with someone else (Hartley with the Muppets, for instance).*

THIRD CHANNEL

Rural Escapes

Spies and Super Sleuths

Fantasy and Science Fiction

The Sixties in Review

Rural Escapes

1. What was the source of the Clampett fortune in *The Beverly Hillbillies*?

2. Name the pig that stole the show on *Green Acres.*

3. Billie Jo, Betty Jo, Bobbie Jo, and Uncle Joe were all part of what spin-off from *The Beverly Hillbillies*?

4. Who did Katy, *The Farmer's Daughter,* first work for as a governess and then eventually marry?

5. What state did the McCoys leave when they moved to California's San Fernando Valley?

6. After the castaways of *Gilligan's Island* were rescued in a two-part special for NBC in 1978, where did they eventually end up?

7. What two series shared a common location (Hooterville) and even some of the same characters?

8. When Andy Griffith left his Mayberry series in 1968, the program continued without him. What was the new title and who was the new lead?

9. Who replaced Gomer Pyle at the Mayberry gas station when he enlisted in the U.S. Marines?

10. After five seasons of *Gomer Pyle, U.S.M.C.,* Jim Nabors went directly into another series. What was it?

11. Who was the CBS executive generally considered to be the chief force behind the early 1960s slant toward rural-oriented sitcoms?

12. After frequent guest shots on *The Smothers Brothers*

Comedy Hour, what pop-country singer earned his own CBS good-time music series?

13. The most unlikely copy of *Rowan and Martin's Laugh-In* was also the most successful, substituting deep-fried country corn for urban-oriented topicality. What was the show?

14. Who was the original narrator of *The Dukes of Hazzard?*

15. How did Sheriff Lobo end up working for a big-city police force?

16. After playing a deputy at a small southern town's police force in ABC's *Carter Country,* Guich Koock went over to an NBC sitcom as co-owner of a bar in another small southern town. Name the series and his partner.

17. Who were the co-producers of *Palmerstown, U.S.A.,* the story of an integrated small southern town during the Depression?

18. What hit series did *Enos* spin off from?

19. Former Los Angeles Rams star Merlin Olsen went from a supporting role in *Little House on the Prairie* to a lead role in what other series produced by Michael Landon?

20. What 1967 CBS series and 1977 NBC series both featured giant grizzly bears named Ben?

BACK IN A MINUTE

for the answers to "Rural Escapes"
But first . . .

The most popular and longest-lasting of the rural-based escapist sitcoms of the 1960s was CBS's *The Beverly Hillbillies.* The program premiered at the end of September 1962, and in little more than a month became the most popular TV show in the country. In reaching number one, *The Beverly Hillbillies* returned sitcoms to the lead spot in the TV ratings, following a five-year period in which Westerns such as *Gunsmoke,* *Wagon Train*, and *Bonanza* had each taken turns at the top.

The Beverly Hillbillies stayed as number one for two years. Then, oddly, the program dropped out of the top ten completely when CBS moved it to a time period only thirty minutes earlier in the evening. (In the meantime, *Bonanza* reclaimed the ratings crown for Westerns.) Fickle TV fans took almost a year to return to the Clampetts in sufficient numbers to bring *The Beverly Hillbillies* back to the top ten. From that point on, though, the show proved remarkably consistent, remaining in the lower portion of the top ten until the summer of 1969. Finally, as part of CBS's rural housecleaning in 1971, the Clampetts were put out to pasture.

ANSWERS

1. *The Clampetts discovered oil on their land in the Ozarks.*

2. *Arnold.*

3. Petticoat Junction.

4. *Congressman Glen Morley (William Windom).*

5. *West Virginia.*

6. *Back on the same island, once again marooned. That special was so successful that they were rescued again. In that sequel, however, they decided to stay on the island anyway and run it as a resort—backed by Thurston Howell's money.*

7. Petticoat Junction *and* Green Acres.

8. Mayberry, R.F.D. *Ken Berry became the new lead character, the soft-spoken Sam Jones.*

9. *Cousin Goober Pyle (George Lindsey).*

10. The Jim Nabors Show, *an hour-long musical variety series for CBS.*

11. *James T. Aubrey.*

12. *Glen Campbell.*

13. Hee-Haw.

14. *Waylon Jennings. He eventually relinquished the task of voice-over episode narration, though his rendition of the title song continued to open each show.*

15. *The state's governor misread the low crime statistics for Lobo's area as a sign of the sheriff's competency. (Actually, Lobo had never bothered to send updated information to the state capital.) As*

a reward, Lobo and his deputies were appointed to a special police task force in Atlanta, Georgia.

16. Lewis and Clark, *with Gabe Kaplan as Stewart Lewis. Guich Koock played Roscoe Clark.*

17. *Norman Lear and Alex Haley.*

18. The Dukes of Hazzard.

19. Father Murphy.

20. Gentle Ben *played on CBS in 1967.* The Life and Times of Grizzly Adams *played on NBC in 1977.*

Spies and Super Sleuths

1. The first dramatization of a James Bond adventure took place on television in 1954 as part of CBS's *Climax* drama anthology. What story was done and who played the role of Bond?

2. What British series featured Roger Moore as international adventurer Simon Templar? Who assumed the role in a late 1970s British revival of the show?

3. Britain's hour-long *Danger Man* espionage series was brought to the United States in 1965 and given a new title and a catchy new opening theme. Name the star, the series, and the artist who sang the top-ten title song.

4. From the early 1960s through its revival in the late 1970s, Britain's *Avengers* featured a half dozen different characters as partners to Patrick Macnee's John Steed. Who were the only two never seen by American audiences?

5. Patrick McGoohan's follow-up project to the adventures of secret agent John Drake was *The Prisoner,* in which he was trapped in a paradise prison. What was the place called?

6. In *The Prisoner,* every character was given a number instead of a name. What was McGoohan's number? Who was number 2? Who was number 1?

7. Who was the female private eye with a pet ocelot, a beauty mark, and devastating skills in karate and judo?

8. What bumbling spy had to dial a telephone in his shoe in order to contact headquarters?

9. What did U.N.C.L.E. and T.H.R.U.S.H. stand for?

10. Who was *The Girl From U.N.C.L.E.*?

11. In *The Wild, Wild West,* who was the dwarflike evil genius who proved to be the greatest foe of agents West and Gordon?

12. *I Spy* set itself apart from the other TV spy shows by filming on location throughout the world. What cover jobs did the lead characters have in the series to explain their constant travel?

13. Nearly thirteen years after *I Spy,* Robert Culp played another gung-ho government agent. Name that 1980s series and his unusual new companion.

14. What TV sleuth would turn to the camera before revealing the identity of that week's killer and ask viewers whether *they* had solved the mystery yet?

15. NBC's 1968 made-for-TV movie, *Prescription: Murder,* served as the original pilot film for what popular 1970s detective series?

16. Who composed the theme music that accompanied the adventures of Peter Gunn and Mr. Lucky?

17. What series featured Sebastian Cabot as Carl Hyatt, a professor of criminology and a special consultant to detectives Don Corey and Jed Sills?

18. Robert Loggia starred as T.H.E. Cat, a reformed cat burglar who fought crime. What did the initials T.H.E. stand for?

19. Who played master thief Alister Mundy, father to Alexander Mundy on *It Takes a Thief?*

20. When *The Man from U.N.C.L.E.* ended its run in January

1968, the series was replaced by *Rowan and Martin's Laugh-In*. What *U.N.C.L.E.* star made a guest appearance (in character) on the first episode of the new variety show?

ANSWERS

1. Casino Royale, *Ian Fleming's first James Bond book. Barry Nelson played Bond.*

2. The Saint. *Ian Ogilvy assumed the role in* The Return of the Saint, *aired in the U.S. on* The CBS Late Movie.

3. *Patrick McGoohan in Secret Agent. Johnny Rivers sang the hit song.*

4. *The first two, Dr. David Keel (Ian Hendry) and Mrs. Catherine Gale (Honor Blackman). However, Ian Hendry did appear in an episode of* The New Avengers *called "To Catch a Rat," a well-done homage to the original partnership that featured Hendry playing another character, a British agent who had worked with John Steed in the early 1960s. The episodes aired in the U.S. featured Emma Peel (Diana Rigg) and Tara King (Linda Thorson) in* The Avengers *and Purdey (Joanna Lumley) and Mike Gambit (Gareth Hunt) in* The New Avengers.

5. *The Village.*

6. *Patrick McGoohan was number 6. Number 2 changed each week, though Leo McKern appeared most often in the role. The last episode of the series revealed that number 1 was, in reality, McGoohan's character as well.*

7. *Honey West, played by Anne Francis.*

8. *Maxwell Smart, Agent 86, played by Don Adams.*

9. *U.N.C.L.E. stood for the United Network Command for Law and Enforcement. In the television series, there was never a similar initial code for Thrush. The series of authorized original U.N.C.L.E. paperback novels, however, identified T.H.R.U.S.H. as the Technological Hierarchy for the Removal of Undesirables and the Subjugation of Humanity.*

10. *Technically there were two. In the 1966 pilot episode ("The Moonglow Affair") aired on* The Man from U.N.C.L.E., *Mary Ann Mobley had the role. For the regular series, though, Stephanie Powers starred as April Dancer—assisted by Noel Harrison as Mark Slate.*

11. *Dr. Miguelito Loveless, played by Michael Dunn.*

12. *Kelly Robinson (Robert Culp) was an international tennis star, and Alexander Scott (Bill Cosby) was his trainer.*

13. The Greatest American Hero *featured Robert Culp as F.B.I. agent Bill Maxwell. William Katt played Ralph Hinkley, a super-powered high-school teacher who worked with him on his cases.*

14. *Ellery Queen.*

15. Columbo.

16. *Henry Mancini.*

17. Checkmate.

18. *The character's name, Thomas Hewitt Edward (T.H.E.). Cat was his surname.*

19. *Fred Astaire. A decade later, Universal Studios attempted to bring Astaire's class to another of its series,* Battlestar: Galactica, *by casting him as the long-lost father of Starbuck.*

20. *Leo G. Carroll as Alexander Waverly, who popped up as a busboy in a party sketch, calling in a message to Napoleon Solo and Illya Kuryakin that he had "found Thrush headquarters."*

Fantasy and Science Fiction

1. Who was the producer responsible for the larger-than-life adventures in *Land of the Giants, Voyage to the Bottom of the Sea,* and *Lost in Space?*

2. Which TV "monster" family featured an unattached hand that popped up throughout the house, a cadaveric butler, and a husband who went mad with passion whenever his wife spoke French?

3. Who were the two actors who looked so much alike in the role of Darrin Stephens on *Bewitched* that viewers suspected a touch of magic at work in the casting office?

4. How did brother Tom acquire supernatural powers on the Smothers Brothers sitcom series?

5. Who was responsible for causing the Robinson family's spaceship to become "lost in space"?

6. What grim reassurance did "the control voice" issue at the beginning of *The Outer Limits?*

7. In the original *Star Trek* pilot, who was the captain of *The Enterprise?*

8. Unlike the spaceships of other TV space series, *The Enterprise* on *Star Trek* never landed on any planet. Why?

9. Who supplied the voices for the 1973 Saturday morning animated cartoon version of *Star Trek?*

10. In *The Invaders,* how could informed earthlings identify the humanlike aliens bent on conquering their planet?

11. What Ray Bradbury short story appeared as an episode of *The Twilight Zone* in the 1960s and as an offering on NBC's *Peacock Showcase* in the 1980s?

12. "Did you ever have the urge to jump?" was the promotional ad tease for what spooky ABC series of the late 1950s?

13. Since its inception in 1963, the British science-fiction series *Dr. Who* cast five different performers in the lead role of the Doctor. Which three once teamed up in the same story?

14. How did Captain Nice and Mr. Terrific acquire their respective super powers?

15. What two different formats were used in the one-season run of the time travel sitcom, *It's About Time*?

16. What made the visit to 1941 Pearl Harbor so unsettling for Dr. Tony Newman (James Darren) in *The Time Tunnel*?

17. How does Mr. Roarke make his customers' dreams come true on *Fantasy Island*?

18. What hardworking reporter for the Chicago-based Independent News Service pursued stories about such subjects as vampires, zombies, Jack the Ripper, and alien invaders?

19. What NBC series featured former Doublemint chewing gum twins Cyb and Tricia Barnstable as the radio crew to a garbage ship in the United Galaxy Sanitation Patrol?

20. Who was the host of ABC's suspense anthology of the early 1980s, *Darkroom*?

ANSWERS

1. *Irwin Allen.*

2. The Addams Family.

3. *Dick York played the role from 1964 to 1969. Dick Sargent took over for the final three seasons of the series.*

4. *Tom died at sea and then returned as an inept but superpowered apprentice angel who made life difficult for his brother, Dick.*

5. *Dr. Zachary Smith (Jonathan Harris) sabotaged the* Jupiter II, *but at takeoff found himself trapped aboard as well. He spent the three-season run of* Lost in Space *scheming a way to get home to Earth.*

6. *The deep-voiced announcer issued this warning: "There is nothing wrong with your television set. We are controlling transmission. We control the vertical. We control the horizontal. For the next hour, we will control all that you see and hear."*

7. *Captain Christopher Pike, played by Jeffrey Hunter.*

8. *The* Enterprise *had not been equipped to land on a planet, lacking both the design and shielding to withstand the effects of gravity and atmospheric friction. In fact, the huge ship had been built in space, so it had never taken off from a planet's surface. From a practical production viewpoint, keeping* The Enterprise *in orbit around each story's planet eliminated boring takeoff and landing sequences.*

9. *Members of the original cast including William Shatner as Captain James T. Kirk; Leonard Nimoy as Mr. Spock; DeForest Kelley as Dr. Leonard McCoy; Nichelle Nichols as Lieutenant Uhura; James Doohan as chief engineer Scotty; George Takei as Mr. Sulu; and Majel Barrett as Nurse Chapel. Walter Koenig's Ensign Chekov was not in the cartoon series.*

10. *The aliens had no heartbeat or pulse, but it was not very safe to get close enough to check. From a distance a few odd traits were visible: some of the aliens had strangely shaped hands marred by such features as a little finger sticking out at an unnatural angle; some of the aliens glowed briefly when their human form weakened; and all of them disintegrated into a pile of ashes when killed.*

11. *"I Sing the Body Electric," the story of a loving robot grand-mother.*

12. One Step Beyond, *hosted by John Newland.*

13. *The first three: William Hartnell, Patrick Troughton, and Jon Pertwee. Appropriately, this 1972 tale was called "The Three Doc-tors." Beyond this story, which involved all three actually working together against an alien menace, there were brief flashback se-quences incorporated into other adventures, but these served chiefly as background footnotes (as in 1982's "Earthshock" with Peter Davison, which included segments with Hartnell, Troughton, and Tom Baker).*

14. *Police chemist Carter Nash (William Daniels) swallowed some super juice liquid that turned him into Captain Nice. Gas station op-erator Stanley Beamish (Stephen Strimpell) swallowed a top-secret U.S. government power pill that turned him into Mr. Terrific.*

15. *In the program's first half of the season, two U.S. astronauts found themselves back in the Stone Age, where they had to cope with Neanderthal life, aided by a friendly cave family. In the second half, the astronauts returned to their own time period, bringing along the cave family which, in turn, had to cope with modern-day life in America.*

16. *Aware of the impending Japanese attack on Pearl Harbor, Tony Newman met his father as a young man there and even caught a glimpse of himself as a child.*

17. *Through magic. Mr. Roarke is really a wizard who conjures up the fantasies each week.*

18. *Carl Kolchak (Darren McGavin) on the series Kolchak: The* Night Stalker.

19. Quark. One was a clone of the other, and they constantly argued about who was the original and who was the clone.

20. James Coburn.

The Sixties in Review

1. Carl Reiner's original pilot for the story of TV writer Rob Petrie was called "Head of the Family," with an entirely different cast from the later *Dick Van Dyke Show*. Who played the character of Rob in this earlier version?

2. What five symbols were used to open *Ben Casey*?

3. Who played an honest cop who happened to be filthy rich?

4. Name the issue-oriented CBS drama series that featured a Manhattan social worker.

5. Who produced the ABC series that offered eager young singles the opportunity to win a blind date with one of three partners hidden behind a studio screen?

6. Name the 1960 sports program that had Milton Berle as host.

7. Who launched an unsuccessful bid for the presidency of the United States on *The Smothers Brothers Comedy Hour*?

8. What successful presidential candidate said "Sock it to me?" on *Rowan and Martin's Laugh-In*?

9. In one of the first made-for-TV movies, *Doomsday Flight,* a mad bomber planted an altitude-sensitive explosive set to detonate whenever the plane dropped below a height of 4,000 feet. How did the plane land safely?

10. Who supplied the voices for the animated series *Calvin and the Colonel*?

11. In what year did NBC become the first network to air all of its prime-time shows in color?

12. On May 1, 1967, a fourth commercial network launched its one-and-only series, *The Las Vegas Show.* Within a month, both the series and the network were gone. What was the network called and who was the host of the series?

13. Who was the mellow-voiced announcer who welcomed viewers to beautiful downtown Burbank for *Rowan and Martin's Laugh-In*?

14. One unsuccessful copy of *Laugh-In* earned the dubious honor of having the shortest run of any network series: one episode. Name the show.

15. What was the first prime-time series in the United States to show the Beatles?

16. On an episode of *The Dick Van Dyke Show,* what real-life rock 'n' roll duo played visiting English superstars who were hidden at the Petrie household before a performance?

17. Which of the members of *Hogan's Heroes*: became a regular on *Laugh-In?* hosted a popular game show? became a TV director on a number of adventure series?

18. Why did *Let's Make a Deal* move to ABC in 1968 after four years on NBC?

19. What did Richard Benjamin's Dick Hollister character do for a living on *He and She*?

20. When he left New York City, where did Jackie Gleason take his Saturday-night comedy-variety show?

ANSWERS

1. *Carl Reiner. For* The Dick Van Dyke Show, *he stepped more into the background and played Alan Brady, star of the show Rob Petrie worked for.*

2. *Man. Woman. Birth. Death. Infinity.*

3. *Gene Barry played the millionaire police captain Amos Burke in* Burke's Law *on* ABC.

4. East Side, West Side, *starring George C. Scott as Manhattan social worker Neil Brock. Cicely Tyson played his secretary, Jane Foster.*

5. *Chuck Barris produced* The Dating Game, *a 1960s update of* Blind Date *from the 1940s.*

6. Jackpot Bowling. *Berle would open and close the show, provide transition patter, and hand out the prize money to the winning bowlers.*

7. *Pat Paulsen.*

8. *Richard Nixon.*

9. *The plane set down in Denver, Colorado, the "mile high" city (5,280 feet above sea level).*

10. *The creators of Amos and Andy. Freeman Gosden did the Colonel (a fast-talking fox) and Charles Correll did Calvin (a kind-hearted but gullible bear).*

11. *The fall of 1966.*

12. *The United Network, nicknamed Uni Net. Bill Dana hosted the ill-fated Las Vegas Show.*

13. *Gary Owens.*

14. Turn-On, *which aired February 5, 1969.*

15. *NBC's* Jack Paar Show, *on January 3, 1964.*

16. *Chad and Jeremy.*

17. *Both Larry Hovis (who played Sergeant Carter) and Richard Dawson (who played Corporal Newkirk) served stints on* Rowan and Martin's Laugh-In. *Richard Dawson also went on to host the popular 1970s game show,* Family Feud. *Ivan Dixon (who played Corporal Kinch) developed his expertise behind the camera, directing episodes of a number of series over the years, including* Bret Maverick *and* The Greatest American Hero *in 1982.*

18. *ABC, which had few hit series, was willing to provide* Let's Make a Deal *with a regular prime-time slot in addition to its daytime spot. NBC wanted the program only in its daytime slot.*

19. *Dick Hollister was a cartoonist who created the character of Jetman. He drew the comic-strip feature and also served as an adviser to the television adaptation.*

20. *Miami Beach, "the sun and fun capital of the world."*

NEWS, WEATHER, AND SPORTS BREAK

News, Weather, and Sports Break

1. Who was WJM-TV's weatherman and why did he leave the station?

2. What baseball milestone took place on NBC's first Monday-night game of the 1974 baseball season?

3. What boxer died shortly after being knocked out, live, on ABC's *Fight of the Week,* on March 17, 1962?

4. Which was the first network to bring National Football League games into prime time?

5. In the fall of 1954, when ABC televised the N.C.A.A. college football games and DuMont carried the N.F.L. pro games, what other professional football league did NBC carry?

6. In what year did ABC first present a series of prime-time National Football League games with Howard Cosell as anchor?

7. On July 11, 1974, an ad-hoc network of 110 stations began regular Thursday-night coverage of a new football league. What was it called?

8. The first football superbowl in 1967 was not only a clash between rival leagues but also a ratings battle between NBC and CBS, both of which carried the game. Who won the game and the ratings contest?

9. Who were the original play-by-play announcers for ABC's *Monday Night Football* series?

10. What was the first network weekend sports anthology series?

11. What were the first Olympic contests anywhere in the world to be televised?

12. The 1972 Olympics in Berlin were unexpectedly transformed from a major sports event to a dramatic news story on Tuesday morning, September 5. What happened?

13. Since 1946, only three men have held the job as chief anchor for the CBS nightly news. Name them.

14. In late 1956, who replaced John Cameron Swayze on NBC's nightly news program?

15. During the live television coverage of the crime hearings conducted by Senator Estes Kefauver in 1951, witness Frank Costello refused to allow the TV cameras to show his face while he testified. What did the networks show instead?

16. What U.S. president held the first live television news conference?

17. In early 1966, CBS opted not to cover, live, one day of congressional hearings on the government's handling of the Vietnam War. Who resigned in protest over this decision?

18. What other post did Roone Arledge hold (and retain) when he was appointed president of ABC News in 1977?

19. What was the first network to begin inserting a sixty-second news summary into prime time?

20. The late-night series *ABC Nightline* evolved out of ABC's coverage of what continuing story that began in late 1979?

BACK IN A MINUTE

**for the answers to "News, Weather, and Sports Break"
But first . . .**

Some Questions Even We Can't Answer:

How come the castaways on *Gilligan's Island* had so many personal belongings with them for a three-hour cruise?

With no money and no IDs, how did The Fugitive always manage to find a job?

Why wasn't the doctor who diagnosed Paul Bryan as terminal in *Run For Your Life* sued for malpractice?

Who at NASA was responsible for hiring the astronauts in *It's About Time* and *I Dream of Jeannie*?

How did Hogan's Heroes manage to sneak all their equipment into a prisoner of war camp?

ANSWERS

1. *Gordy Howard (John Amos) played WJM-TV's weatherman on* The Mary Tyler Moore Show. *He left the station for a network job as a celebrity interviewer.*

2. *On April 8, 1974, Hank Aaron hit his 715th career home run, breaking Babe Ruth's record.*

3. *Benny "Kid" Paret, who was knocked out by Emile Griffith.*

4. *DuMont. On October 3, 1953, DuMont aired its first regular "game of the week," in which the Pittsburgh Steelers beat the New York Giants 24 to 14.*

5. *The Canadian Pro Football League.*

6. *1959. The games ran from 10:30 P.M. to 1:00 A.M. on Saturday nights from August through October.*

7. *The World Football League.*

8. *The National Football League's Green Bay Packers beat the American Football League's Kansas City Chiefs 35 to 10. CBS (television home of the N.F.L.) beat NBC (television home of the A.F.L.) in the Nielsen ratings, 24.6 to 17.4.*

9. *Howard Cosell, Keith Jackson, and color man "Dandy" Don Meredith.*

10. The CBS Sports Spectacular, *which premiered in January 1960.*

11. *The 1936 Olympics in Berlin were carried by Germany's new electronic television system to twenty-eight public viewing rooms.*

12. *Palestinian terrorists captured a group of Israeli athletes inside the Olympic compound and held them as hostages. The crisis ended some twelve hours later with a violent airport shoot-out between police and the terrorists that left all the hostages dead.*

13. *Douglas Edwards, Walter Cronkite, and Dan Rather.*

14. *Chet Huntley and David Brinkley.*

15. *The network cameras focused only on his hands. Ironically, Costello attracted much more attention than he would have if he had routinely testified as the other witnesses did.*

16. *President John F. Kennedy, on January 25, 1961.*

17. *Fred Friendly, then the head of CBS News.*

18. *Roone Arledge was also president of ABC's sports operation, traditionally regarded as quite different from the news division. Nonetheless, he did well in both positions.*

19. *NBC, which instituted* NBC News Update *on August 6, 1975.*

20. *The seizure of the American embassy in Iran and the capture of more than fifty people who were subsequently held as hostages. ABC provided daily late-night coverage of the story under the banner* The Iran Crisis: America Held Hostage, *building a solid audience for an in-depth late-night news program. In March 1980 the program was rechristened* Nightline *and expanded in scope to cover other stories besides the hostage situation in Iran.*

FOURTH CHANNEL
Urban Escapes
Public Broadcasting
Sex and Violence
The Seventies in Review

Urban Escapes

1. In a break from the usual Los Angeles setting, both *The Mary Tyler Moore Show* and *The Bob Newhart Show* were located in midwestern cities. Name them.

2. Who was the doorman at Rhoda's apartment building in New York City?

3. How did marshal Sam McCloud stand out in the streets of New York City?

4. In the urban crime series *Longstreet,* what handicap did the title character have?

5. When Mike and Gloria first moved out of Archie and Edith's house into a home of their own, where did they go?

6. How did George Jefferson make his fortune?

7. How did the book *Blood on the Badge* tie in with the characters of *Barney Miller*?

8. What did Fish do when he retired from Barney Miller's precinct?

9. How and why did the character of James Evans die in *Good Times*?

10. Why had WKRP's Dr. Johnny Fever been fired from his big-money job at a Los Angeles radio station?

11. What business were Chico and "the man" in?

12. Who played the tyrannical law professor, Charles Kingsfield, in both the television series and the feature-film version of *The Paper Chase*?

13. Why did Gabe Kotter decide to teach at Buchanan High School?

14. At the end of *The White Shadow*'s second season, the Carver High School basketball team advanced to the city championship finals. Where did they finish?

15. Who played Chet Kincaid, a physical-education teacher and coach at a Los Angeles high school?

16. *Police Woman, Joe Forrester,* and *David Cassidy—Man Undercover* were all spin-offs from what anthology series?

17. ABC's late 1970s sitcom, *Makin' It,* was closely connected with what hit theatrical film?

18. How did NBC attempt to carry on *Sanford and Son* after both Redd Foxx and Demond Wilson left the series?

19. What went wrong with WKRP's big Thanksgiving Day remote broadcast from a local shopping mall?

20. What job did Anthony Quinn's character have in *Man and the City*?

BACK IN A MINUTE

for the answers to "Urban Escapes"
But first . . .

The tremendous changes in entertainment styles during the 1970s are best illustrated by comparing the top ten TV shows at the start of the decade with the equivalent list at the end.

As the 1970s began, the following shows and stars were in the top ten: Ed Sullivan (on since 1948), Red Skelton and Lucille Ball (on since 1951), *Gunsmoke* and Walt Disney's show (on since 1954), *Bonanza* (on since 1959), *My Three Sons* (on since 1960), and *Mayberry, R.F.D.*, the continuation of *The Andy Griffith Show*, which had been on since 1960.

As the 1970s ended, the top ten was filled with such relative newcomers as *Three's Company* (on since 1977), *Dallas*, *Fantasy Island*, and *Taxi* (on since 1978), and *The Dukes of Hazzard* and *Real People* (on since 1979). The oldest top ten show was *60 Minutes*, which had begun in 1968 but had spent five years outside prime time. After that came *M*A*S*H*, which had premiered in 1972.

ANSWERS

1. The Mary Tyler Moore Show *was set in Minneapolis, and* The Bob Newhart Show *was set in Chicago.*

2. *Carlton, played by Lorenzo Music. The character was never seen, only heard—usually through the apartment building's intercom system.*

3. *McCloud wore a cowboy hat and frequently rode his horse through the city streets.*

4. *Insurance investigator Mike Longstreet (James Franciscus) was blind.*

5. *Next door, into the house previously occupied by the Jefferson family.*

6. *George Jefferson ran a successful dry-cleaning business that he expanded into a chain.*

7. *In the series story line,* Blood on the Badge *was the name of the successful novel written by the character of Ron Harris (Ron Glass). Harris drew from experiences at the 12th Precinct, so many of the characters in that fictitious book bore a striking resemblance to his co-workers.*

8. *Phil Fish and his wife, Bernice, became foster parents to five urban street kids.*

9. *James Evans (John Amos) died off camera in an auto accident in Mississippi. The character was written out when John Amos left the program after the third season, citing his personal dissatisfaction with the story and character development, especially the emphasis placed on the antics of J. J.*

10. *Johnny Fever had said "booger" on the air.*

11. *They operated a small garage in East Los Angeles.*

12. *John Houseman.*

13. *Kotter had gone to the school himself and recognized the importance of taking the time to provide the hard-core "problem" students with at least the basics of a high-school education.*

14. *First.*

15. *Bill Cosby, in his half-hour sitcom,* The Bill Cosby Show.

16. NBC's Police Story.

17. Saturday Night Fever. Makin' It *drew inspiration from the film for: the central premise of a talented disco dancer; Bee Gees music for the dance sequences; a real-life hit as the title song; and even another Travolta (Ellen, not John).*

18. *NBC renamed the program* The Sanford Arms, *building on the fact that Fred and Lamont had previously set up a boardinghouse next door to their junk yard. The characters of Aunt Esther (La-Wanda Page) and Grady Wilson (Whitman Mayo) from* Sanford and Son *stuck around for the new series, but it folded after only one month.*

19. *As a promotional stunt, Arthur Carlson and Herb Tarlek released live turkeys from a helicopter over a shopping-center parking lot, not realizing that the birds were unable to fly. The turkeys crashed to the ground as a horrified Les Nessman described the event, live, over the air.*

20. *Quinn's Thomas Alcala character was mayor of a small southwestern city.*

Public Broadcasting

1. Though the FCC set aside frequences for noncommercial educational stations back in 1952, it left one important aspect of the system unsettled. What was it?

2. How did public television originally distribute its programs to stations across the country?

3. Before being called PBS, how was the Public Broadcasting System identified?

4. To raise needed operating cash, San Francisco's KQED instituted an annual fund-raising event in the early 1950s. What was it?

5. One of the first quasi-hits on public television was a cooking show produced by WGBH in Boston. Name the show and its host.

6. On June 25, 1967, public television stations in the United States linked into the first truly worldwide television show, *Our World.* What hit recording by the Beatles received its world premiere airing on this broadcast?

7. *PBL,* the *Public Broadcasting Laboratory,* was public television's first slick documentary-feature program, and it spurred the creation of a similar show on CBS the following season. Name that show.

8. One of public television's first big hit British historical drama imports was an expensive adaptation of works by John Galsworthy. What was the series?

9. What was the first *Masterpiece Theater* series?

10. What 1975 CBS series attempted to cash in on the popularity of *Upstairs, Downstairs* with a similar period drama set in Boston?

11. Name the controversial play shown on PBS's *Hollywood Television Theater* in 1973, which offered a rather unusual portrait of the afterlife, presenting God as a Puerto Rican bath attendant.

12. What public-television series incorporated some flashy techniques from commercial television to catch the attention of youthful viewers, even identifying as "sponsors" various letters of the alphabet?

13. Name the economics reporter from ABC News who came over to PBS to host *Wall Street Week*.

14. What talk-show host went from ABC to CBS to NBC to public television in less than three years?

15. What American commercial network did Robert MacNeil anchor for prior to the *MacNeil-Lehrer Report*?

16. What British comedy series featured Monty Python veteran John Cleese as the manager of a small rural hotel?

17. What was public television's weekly guide to the movies, and who were its original co-hosts?

18. Who sang the theme song to PBS's country-music series, *Austin City Limits*?

19. In the late 1970s, PBS began late-evening rebroadcasts of one commercial network's evening news show, adding captions for the hearing impaired. What network supplied the program each day?

20. Who exposed PBS viewers to an elementary course in astronomy while exploring the wonders of the cosmos?

ANSWERS

1. *Funding. It was not clear where operating cash for noncommercial stations that were independent of the government would come from.*

2. *Through the U.S. mail.*

3. *First as the Educational Television and Radio Center, then as National Educational Television (NET).*

4. *An on-air auction. During the 1950s, this ploy was practical only for public-television stations on the VHF band. Unfortunately, most were on the rarely viewed UHF band.*

5. The French Chef, *with Julia Child.*

6. *"All You Need is Love."*

7. 60 Minutes.

8. The Forsyte Saga.

9. The First Churchills, *which ran in January, 1971.*

10. Beacon Hill.

11. Steambath.

12. Sesame Street.

13. *Louis Rukeyser.*

14. *Dick Cavett. Cavett ended his late-night ABC talk show on January 1, 1975; hosted a four-week variety series for CBS during the summer of 1975; and then served as a floating backup performer for NBC (popping up on Saturday Night Live and as host to NBC's first Big Event telecast, "The Big Party"). In the fall of 1977, he revived his talk show format for PBS.*

15. *NBC. He co-anchored* The Scherer-MacNeil Report.

16. Fawlty Towers.

17. Sneak Previews, *hosted by Gene Siskel and Roger Ebert. In the fall of 1982 they left the program for a similar show syndicated on commercial television,* At The Movies, *while Jeffrey Lyons and Neal Gabler took over on* Sneak Previews.

18. *The Lost Gonzo Band, which sang "London Homesick Blues."*

19. *ABC, which provided copies of its* World News Tonight *program.*

20. *Carl Sagan on* Cosmos.

Sex and Violence

1. What did S.W.A.T. stand for?

2. Who starred in the television series version of the hit theatrical film *Shaft*?

3. Name the street-wise L.A. cop who was a master of disguise and owner of a pet cockatoo.

4. Name the confident bald New York police detective with an explosive temper and a lollipop.

5. What happened at the climax of the controversial 1974 made-for-TV film *Born Innocent* starring Linda Blair?

6. In NBC's *James at 15,* what happened to the lead character when he turned sixteen?

7. Both *Love, American Style* and *The Love Boat* were comedy anthologies consisting of three or four different stories each week. What was the key difference in how the stories on the two series unfolded?

8. What film trick was used to stylize the violent confrontations in such kiddie adventure series as *Kung Fu, The Six Million Dollar Man,* and *The Incredible Hulk?*

9. What program running opposite *Charlie's Angels* in 1978 playfully christened four beautiful women in its cast as "Pappy's Lambs"?

10. What was the chief effect of all the angry protests and pre-broadcast publicity surrounding the premiere of *Soap*?

11. In *Soap,* who were the parents of the baby possessed by the devil but subsequently exorcised by Jessica Tate and the rest of the family?

12. Name the Larry Gelbart comedy series (reminiscent of Ingmar Bergman's *Scenes from a Marriage*) that devoted most of each episode to conversations between a husband and wife about life, death, and sex.

13. ABC's late 1960s series *The Ugliest Girl in Town* and early 1980s series *Bosom Buddies* both shared the same gimmick hook. What was it?

14. What was the actual marital status of the two main characters in the mid-1960s NBC sitcom *Occasional Wife?*

15. Who was the first leader of the Impossible Missions Force?

16. In the first season of his series, Joe Mannix worked for a detective firm called Intertect. Who was his boss?

17. *Undercover Woman,* the show-within-a-show on Betty White's 1977 sitcom, was a sly allusion to what popular NBC cop series running at the time?

18. What painful decision faced by Maude in the program's first season touched off a wave of protests?

19. What leading lady of a 1960s sitcom became involved in a controversy over whether or not to show her belly button?

20. Where did the one-and-only romantic encounter between *M*A*S*H*'s Hawkeye Pierce and Margaret Houlihan take place?

ANSWERS

1. *Special Weapons And Tactics.*

2. *Richard Roundtree, who had played the role in the original theatrical films.*

3. *Tony Baretta, played by Robert Blake.*

4. *Theo Kojak, played by Telly Savalas.*

5. *Linda Blair's character, fourteen-year-old Chris Parker, was gang-raped in the shower of a state reform school by a group of girls using a wooden plunger.*

6. *He lost his virginity.*

7. *On Love, American Style each story played as a self-contained segment. The Love Boat, on the other hand, tied each of the individual segments together as part of the same overall story, usually involving the series regulars in transition scenes.*

8. *The action ran in slow motion so that the battle sequences lasted longer and could be seen in greater detail.*

9. Black Sheep Squadron, *a World War II drama on NBC.*

10. Soap *became the most successful new show of the fall of 1977 due to the tremendous publicity boost it had received. In addition, during the first season ABC ran warnings identifying the program as adult-oriented and some affiliates even delayed the broadcast until later in the evening.*

11. *Corrine Tate (Diana Canova) and Tim Flotsky (Sal Viscuso), a former priest.*

12. United States.

13. *Dressing the male lead characters as women. Tim Blair (Peter*

Kastner) dressed as a woman in The Ugliest Girl in Town *in order to earn passage to London as a model. In* Bosom Buddies, *Kip Wilson (Tom Hanks), and Henry Desmond (Peter Scolari) both dressed as women in order to live in an inexpensive New York City apartment house open only to women.*

14. *They were unattached and lived in separate apartments. The need for an occasional wife was simple: Peter Christopher (Michael Callan) was a young executive at a baby-food corporation that would only promote married men, so he asked Greta Patterson (Patricia Harty), a starving young painter, to pose as his wife. In return, he paid for her art lessons and a separate apartment two flights up.*

15. *Daniel Briggs, played by Steven Hill.*

16. *Lou Wickersham, played by Joe Campanella.*

17. Police Woman, *starring Angie Dickinson.*

18. *Maude discovered she was pregnant and decided to have an abortion.*

19. *Barbara Eden, the star of* I Dream of Jeannie.

20. *Behind enemy lines in an abandoned shack.*

The Seventies in Review

1. What was the first spin-off show from *All in the Family*?

2. What comedy-anthology program presented the pilot episode for *Happy Days?* Ron Howard played Richie, but who played his father?

3. The low-key family drama of *The Waltons* managed to win its tough first-season time slot in 1972 against what NBC variety series and ABC cop show?

4. Name the three people responsible for (respectively) the following flops: *The Dumplings; Me and the Chimp; We'll Get By.*

5. What Tennessee Williams play presented in December 1973 on *ABC Theater* marked the television dramatic debut of Katharine Hepburn?

6. Who was guest narrator on the final episode of CBS's *Bicentennial Minute* program, describing "the way it was" in American history two hundred years earlier?

7. Who played the role of Grandpa in *The Homecoming*, the 1971 made-for-TV film that served as a pilot for *The Waltons?*

8. NBC censors cut the opening to the first episode of Richard Pryor's 1977 variety series. What did it originally consist of?

9. What Jack Webb-produced series did David Janssen star in between *The Fugitive* and *Harry-O?*

10. The first miniseries to play on consecutive nights in prime time focused on the career of a hardworking policeman rapidly approaching retirement age. Name the program.

11. What real-life event inspired the television miniseries *Washington: Behind Closed Doors* and *Blind Ambition*?

12. Soon after his stint in *M*A*S*H,* Wayne Rogers took the role of a 1930s private detective in Los Angeles. Name the series, loosely patterned after the hit theatrical film *Chinatown.*

13. How did the character of Frank Burns leave *M*A*S*H*?

14. In Paddy Chayefsky's 1975 feature film about television, *Network,* Howard Beale urged his viewers to open their windows and vent their anger and frustration with him. What did they shout?

15. Each of the six main supporting characters on *The Mary Tyler Moore Show* went on to star in their own series. Name the performers and their shows.

16. George Schlatter's 1977 revival of *Laugh-In* featured in its supporting cast a then-unknown comic who became a sitcom superstar one year later. Who was it?

17. Norman Lear's 1978 sitcom about a newly elected black congressman, *Mr. Dugan,* earned what dubious honor in TV history?

18. Each of the networks attempted to cash in on the success of *Animal House* with a television equivalent. Which one had the official TV adaptation of the film?

19. What 1979 George Schlatter series for NBC focused on the exploits of "ordinary folks," in the process launching a programming fad labeled "reality shows"?

20. What late 1970s medical documentary series on NBC followed the activities of real-life doctors—including intense scenes in the operating room?

ANSWERS

1. Maude, *featuring Beatrice Arthur as Edith Bunker's upper middle-class cousin.*

2. Love, American Style, *in February 1972, with Harold Gould as Richie's father. The character of Fonzie was not in the pilot.*

3. The Flip Wilson Show *on* NBC *and* The Mod Squad *on* ABC.

4. *Norman Lear supervised production on* The Dumplings *(1976 on* NBC*); Garry Marshall nurtured* Me and the Chimp *(1972 on* CBS*); and Alan Alda created* We'll Get By *(1975 on* CBS*).*

5. The Glass Menagerie.

6. *President Gerald R. Ford.*

7. *Edgar Bergen.*

8. *As Pryor assured the audience that he had not been forced to give up anything in order to perform on television, the camera pulled back to a full body shot revealing him apparently castrated. (Actually, he was wearing a skin-tight body stocking.) In place of this, the first* Richard Pryor Show *ran a graphic saying that the opening skit would not be seen—ever.*

9. O'Hara, U.S. Treasury, *which ran for only the 1971–72 season.*

10. The Blue Knight, *starring William Holden, which aired on* NBC *in November 1973. Two years later,* CBS *ran a regular series version of the story, with George Kennedy as the new lead.*

11. *The* Watergate *scandal, which led to the resignation of President Richard Nixon.*

12. City of Angels.

13. *While in Tokyo following Margaret Houlihan's marriage to an* *army colonel, a depressed Frank Burns went on a binge through many of the city's night spots. Naturally, this led to a promotion and a transfer back to the States.*

14. "*I'm as mad as hell and I'm not going to take it anymore!*"

15. *While* The Mary Tyler Moore Show *was still on, both Valerie Harper and Cloris Leachman won direct spin-off shows featuring their already established characters:* Rhoda *and* Phyllis, *respectively. After* The Mary Tyler Moore Show *ended, Ed Asner took his character into an hour-long drama series,* Lou Grant. *The other series had no direct connection to* The Mary Tyler Moore Show: *Gavin MacLeod on* The Love Boat; *Ted Knight on* Too Close for Comfort *(after the short-lived* Ted Knight Show*); and Betty White on the MTM-produced* Betty White Show. *Even Georgia Engel won a short-run series,* The Goodtime Girls.

16. *Robin Williams, later known as Mork from Ork on* Mork and Mindy.

17. *The program was canceled at the last minute even though it had gotten as far as having promo ads run on CBS, featuring scenes from the already completed episodes. This quick cancellation followed vocal criticism of the premise by real-life black congressmen.*

18. *ABC's* Delta House *was the official TV adaptation of the hit film and even included members of the original cast (although not John Belushi).*

19. Real People.

20. Lifeline.

HEART BREAK

Heart Break

1. Television's first regular soap opera series ran on the Du-Mont television network in 1946. What was it called?

2. What was the first daytime network soap opera?

3. Counting its fifteen-year network radio run, what soap opera became the longest-running network entertainment show in American broadcasting?

4. What was the first daily television soap opera to run: thirty minutes? sixty minutes? ninety minutes?

5. What was the first prime-time drama series to be moved into a daytime soap slot?

6. What mid-1960s ABC soap opera featured two former prime-time child stars: Tony Dow of *Leave it to Beaver* and Tommy Rettig of *Lassie*?

7. What writer was responsible for creating such venerable soaps as *The Guiding Light*, *The Brighter Day*, and *As the World Turns*?

8. During the heyday of ABC's *Peyton Place*, CBS placed into prime time a spin-off from the top-rated daytime soap, *As the World Turns.* Name this twice-weekly series.

9. What did the title *The Edge of Night* originally refer to?

10. What CBS soap opera was interrupted by the first news of John Kennedy's assassination on November 22, 1963?

11. What ABC soap opera of the late 1960s added ghosts, vampires, and werewolves to the usual sudsy plot complications?

12. What prime-time soap opera did NBC revive in 1972 and place in an afternoon slot with a new cast and crew?

13. Name the performer who continued as a central character on *Search for Tomorrow* from its television debut in 1951 into the 1980s.

14. The wedding of *General Hospital*'s Luke and Laura was a 1981 daytime ratings smash. One year later, were the two characters still together?

15. Name the Christian Broadcasting Network's early 1980s venture into soaps.

BACK IN A MINUTE

for the answers to "Heart Break"
But first . . .

Some Questions Even We Can't Answer:

Why wasn't Ted Baxter fired his first day on the job?

Whatever happened to Richie Cunningham's older brother, Chuck?

Where did the Hulk get his changes of clothes?

What was Columbo's first name?

What did "coronet blue" mean? Did Michael Alden ever get his memory back? And why were people trying to kill him in the first place?

ANSWERS

1. Faraway Hill.

2. These Are My Children, *which began in January 1949.*

3. The Guiding Light, *which began on radio in 1937 and came over to television in 1952.*

4. The Edge of Night *ran for thirty minutes beginning in April 1956.* Another World *ran for sixty minutes beginning in January 1975 and then expanded to ninety minutes in March 1979.*

5. Hawkins Falls, Pop. 6,200, *which ran on NBC's prime-time schedule in 1950, then moved to a daytime soap slot in 1951.*

6. Never Too Young.

7. *Irna Phillips.*

8. Our Private World.

9. *The time placement of the soap opera on CBS's late-afternoon schedule (4:30 P.M.)—at the "edge" of night.*

10. As the World Turns.

11. Dark Shadows.

12. Peyton Place, *dubbed* Return to Peyton Place.

13. *Mary Stuart.*

14. *Of course not.*

15. Another Life.

FIFTH CHANNEL

Prime-Time Soaps
Late Night and Overnight
Cable Connections
The Eighties (So Far)

Prime-Time Soaps

1. Who played Allison Mackenzie and Rodney Harrington on ABC's *Peyton Place*?

2. Which of the Ingalls children went blind on *Little House on the Prairie*?

3. At the end of the twelve-year run of *My Three Sons*, how many of the males in the household remained unmarried?

4. What live drama series (based on a hit book, play, and feature film) ran for seven years on CBS, focusing on the complications facing a Norwegian-American family at the turn of the century?

5. What popular NBC medical series of the early 1960s switched from its hour-long format to a twice-weekly soap structure for its final season?

6. What was the name of ABC's late 1960s soap developed by Harold Robbins, which bombed after only a few months on the air?

7. Louise Lasser left *Mary Hartman, Mary Hartman* after its second season. How was her character written out of the series and what was her final scene?

8. Norman Lear's second syndicated soap opera was *All That Glitters*. What was its gimmick hook?

9. Only a few years before *Dallas*, CBS tried another prime-time soap focusing on the sudsy intrigues of the corporate world. Name that flop.

10. Who played Jock Ewing's archrival, Digger Barnes, in the first few episodes of *Dallas*?

11. Who were Jock Ewing's four sons on *Dallas*?

12. Why did Michael Tyrone plot revenge against practically everyone in town on *Flamingo Road*?

13. What soap from Aaron Spelling cast as its ruthless business lord the former voice of Charlie in Spelling's *Charlie's Angels*?

14. How did Joyce Davenport publicly "announce" that she and Frank Furillo were romantically involved in *Hill Street Blues*?

15. What personal problem did both John LaRue and Frank Furillo have to control on *Hill Street Blues*?

BACK IN A MINUTE

for the answers to "Prime Time Soaps"
But first . . .

Some Questions Even We Can't Answer:

Why didn't Charlie ever show his face on *Charlie's Angels*?

How did Klinger become a corporal?

Did *Soap*'s Jessica Tate escape the South American firing squad?

Why do the Dukes of Hazzard still have their driver's licenses?

What if you want only *one* knife?

ANSWERS

1. *Mia Farrow played Allison MacKenzie and Ryan O'Neal played Rodney Harrington.*

2. *Daughter Mary, played by Melissa Sue Anderson.*

3. *Only Ernie (Barry Livingston)—who was still a bit too young—and Uncle Charley (William Demarest) remained unmarried.*

4. *Mama,* which ran from 1949 to 1956, based on I Remember Mama.

5. Dr. Kildare.

6. The Survivors.

7. *Mary Hartman ran off with Sergeant Dennis Foley (Bruce Solomon) but quickly settled into her old routines with him. The final scene with Louise Lasser was a virtual replay of the original opening episode, with Mary Hartman pondering the waxy yellow buildup on her floor while Foley grabbed a beer from the refrigerator.*

8. *All That Glitters had a sexual role reversal setup, operating under the premise that from creation to the present, women had assumed the traditionally male roles and traits—and vice versa.*

9. *Executive Suite,* which had a brief run in the 1976–77 season.

10. *David Wayne, who was succeeded by Keenan Wynn.*

11. *J. R. (Larry Hagman), Bobby (Patrick Duffy), Gary (David Ackroyd, then Ted Shackelford) and Ray Krebbs (Steve Kanaly), Jock's illegitimate son.*

12. *Tyrone felt that they were responsible for the death of his father, either directly or indirectly by quiet compliance.*

13. Dynasty.

14. *In full view of everyone at the precinct house, she stepped into the open doorway of Furillo's glass-enclosed office, embraced him, and gave him a long, passionate kiss. One tactful worker closed the office door behind them.*

15. *Alcoholism. In fact, Furillo was at the first meeting of the alcoholics self-help group that LaRue joined.*

Late Night and Overnight

1. What easygoing singer pioneered the post prime-time hours for NBC in 1949 as host to the late-night *Supper Club*?

2. Who did NBC pick to host its first late-night variety-talk show, *Broadway Open House*?

3. Who was the first host of the *Tonight* show?

4. Who did Johnny Carson succeed as host to the *Tonight* show?

5. By the fall of 1969, all three networks had late-night talk shows running opposite each other. Who were the respective hosts?

6. What young reporter (dubbed "the Jack Paar of the counterculture") earned his own occasional ABC late-night network series, *Good Night, America*, beginning in 1973?

7. What late-night rock series broke new ground in 1973 by starting at 1:00 A.M. Saturday morning, and who was the chief announcer?

8. What was NBC's post-*Tonight* talk show, which ran from 1973 to 1982, and who was its host?

9. Who was the guest host on the 1975 premiere of *Saturday Night Live*?

10. Who was the first guest host of ABC's *Fridays*?

11. Though the late-night *SCTV* program for NBC contained a good deal of brand-new material, some of it was actually a few years old. Why?

12. What production company was responsible for *Late Night With David Letterman*?

13. What *Saturday Night Live* cast members were known for their impressions of: Gerald Ford? Jimmy Carter? Barbara Walters? Henry Kissinger? Buckwheat? Frank Sinatra?

14. What late-night news program did Lloyd Dobyns host prior to his stint as an anchor for *NBC Overnight*?

15. What were Joey Bishop's first words on his mid-1960s ABC series that was up against Johnny Carson?

ANSWERS

1. *Perry Como.*

2. *Los Angeles comic Don "Creesh" Hornsby, but he died shortly before the show's scheduled premiere. After some reshuffling, NBC split the hosting chores between Morey Amsterdam (twice a week) and Jerry Lester (the remaining three days).*

3. *Steve Allen.*

4. *Jack Paar.*

5. *Joey Bishop on ABC, Merv Griffin on CBS, and Johnny Carson on NBC.*

6. *Geraldo Rivera.*

7. The Midnight Special, *with rock DJ Wolfman Jack.*

8. Tomorrow, *hosted by Tom Synder.*

9. *George Carlin.*

10. *George Carlin. This was not the first episode of Fridays, however, only the first with a guest host, a policy adopted in the program's second season.*

11. *In order to fill NBC's request for a number of ninety-minute programs virtually overnight in 1981, the SCTV crew incorporated some material from more than seventy half-hour episodes that had been produced for syndication since 1977.*

12. *Johnny Carson's production company.*

13. *Chevy Chase did Gerald Ford; Dan Aykroyd did Jimmy Carter; Gilda Radner did Barbara Walters; John Belushi did Henry Kissinger; Eddie Murphy did Buckwheat; and Joe Piscopo did Frank Sinatra.*

14. Weekend, *a monthly news and public-affairs program that ran from 11:30 P.M.–1:00 A.M. Saturday nights on NBC from 1974 to 1978.*

15. *"Are the ratings out yet?"*

Cable Connections

1. What was America's first "superstation"?

2. What giant electronics firm experimented with pay television in Chicago in the early 1950s?

3. On September 30, 1975, Home Box Office carried its first satellite-fed program, the heavyweight championship bout between what two boxing superstars?

4. What was the key difference between Home Box Office's monthly fee and the billing systems of previous pay TV ventures, such as California's Subscription TV Service in the early 1960s?

5. What sometimes controversial former CBS newsman was one of the original anchors for the first twenty-four-hour television news network?

6. What cable system, first tested in 1977 in Columbus, Ohio, allowed viewers to "talk back" to their sets through their home-control board?

7. In 1981, CBS Cable and Norman Lear revived what popular game show of the 1940s and 1950s?

8. What cable service was the first to devote itself to rock music, programming short video-taped segments and concert specials?

9. Following the success of National Lampoon's *Animal House*, the same group produced an hour-long comedy special for HBO. What was the program called?

10. Who launched the first twenty-four-hour television news network?

11. How did pay TV systems such as ON TV serve cities not yet wired for cable?

12. In 1981, a cultural cable service called ARTS appeared on the Warner Brothers Nickelodeon cable system. What established commercial network was responsible for it?

13. What cable service provided live coverage of the U.S. Congress in session?

14. What was the first twenty-four-hour TV sports network?

15. What cable network outbid PBS in the early 1980s for first-run American rights to all BBC programs?

ANSWERS

1. *Ted Turner's Atlanta station, WTBS (Channel 17). He turned this UHF station into America's first "superstation" by getting it carried by cable systems throughout the country, via satellite.*

2. *Zenith.*

3. *Muhammad Ali and Joe Frazier.*

4. *Previous pay systems had emphasized pay-per-viewing structures in which viewers faced the uncomfortable fact that they would be billed for every program they chose to watch. HBO patterned its billing after services such as the telephone company, which charged a flat monthly rate for maintaining the connection no matter how much or how little it was used. This system gave HBO a more stable source of monthly fees and offered subscribers a predictable monthly bill.*

5. *Daniel Schorr.*

6. *Qube.*

7. The Quiz Kids.

8. *MTV, beginning in 1981.*

9. Disco Beaver from Outer Space.

10. *Ted Turner, with his Cable News Network in June 1980.*

11. *These services sent scrambled signals over existing, available channels (usually on UHF). Home subscribers used a decoder box to unscramble the picture. With no competition from cable, these services generally stuck with uncut theatrical films as programming material.*

12. *ABC.*

13. *The Cable Satellite Public Affairs Network (C-SPAN).*

14. *The Entertainment and Sports Programming Network (ESPN).*

15. *RCA's cable service, The Entertainment Channel.*

The Eighties (So Far)

1. In the fall of 1980, ABC, CBS, and NBC had to begin the new season without new episodes of most of their regular series. Why?

2. What exotic miniseries scored so well over its five-night run in 1980 that it gave NBC the highest-rated week in its history?

3. Why was there controversy concerning Vanessa Redgrave's appearance in the CBS made-for-TV film *Playing for Time*?

4. Who succeeded Fred Silverman as head of NBC?

5. What major error did the networks make while covering the attempted assassination of President Ronald Reagan in 1981?

6. What CBS science series did Walter Cronkite host even after his retirement from the evening news anchor position?

7. The 1980 political nominating conventions were the last anchored on CBS by Walter Cronkite. Which were the first?

8. What dubious honor did *Hill Street Blues* claim in being renewed for a second season?

9. Why did Tony Randall's *Love, Sidney* initially stir up some controversy concerning the lead character?

10. Who played Sebastian in the 1981 PBS presentation of *Brideshead Revisited*?

11. Why was the 1981 ABC movie special *Pray TV* criticized by both supporters and critics of television evangelists?

12. The people behind the hit theatrical film *Airplane!* created a miniseries parody of cop shows for ABC in 1982. What was it called and what inevitably happened to the weekly guest star?

13. When *WKRP in Cincinnati* ended its series run in 1982, where had the station climbed to in the Cincinnati market?

14. What caused a year's delay in two NBC series scheduled for 1981: *The Devlin Connection* and *The Powers of Matthew Star*?

15. Who won the television rights to the 1984 summer Olympic games, to be held in Los Angeles?

ANSWERS

1. *A strike by screen actors earlier in the year (starting in July) had shut down production for the new television season. The dispute was not settled until October, so the 1980–81 season did not really get rolling until well into November.*

2. Shōgun.

3. *Vanessa Redgrave was a vocal supporter of the Palestine Liberation Organization, yet she was chosen to portray a French Jew in a Nazi concentration camp.*

4. *Grant Tinker, previously head of the MTM production company.*

5. *They mistakenly reported that President Reagan's press secretary, James Brady, had died. Though Brady was in fact seriously wounded, he did live.*

6. Universe.

7. *The 1952 conventions.*

8. *That it was one of the lowest-rated network entertainment series ever to be renewed for a second season.*

9. *The character of Sidney Shorr was supposed to be a homosexual. That aspect of the setup was barely even acknowledged once the series began, with Randall emphasizing the more traditional television slant of a loving father or uncle figure to the young mother and daughter sharing his apartment.*

10. *Anthony Andrews, previously known to American audiences as the cad who left The Love Boat's Julie McCoy waiting at the altar.*

11. *Supporters of television evangelists criticized Pray TV even before it hit the air for placing negative emphasis on such areas as*

fund raising and merchandising. Critics of such *TV* preachers complained that the film was far too timid and failed to take a firm stand—possibly even due to pressure brought against the network.

12. Police Squad! *Each week's guest star appeared during the opening credit sequence and would be killed within a few seconds.*

13. *The top ten (number six, to be exact).*

14. *Rock Hudson, star of* The Devlin Connection, *had to undergo heart surgery and needed time to recuperate. Peter Barton was injured in an accident while filming an episode of* The Powers Of Matthew Star. *Both programs premiered in the fall of 1982.*

15. *ABC.*

FADE TO BLACK/ SWITCH OFF

Fade to Black/ Switch Off

1. How did Red Skelton close his program?

2. Though it continued in syndication, *What's My Line* had its last prime-time network broadcast in 1967. Who was the mystery guest on this final episode?

3. For Doctor Richard Kimble, what was the day the running stopped?

4. In Carol Burnett's final appearance as a regular on *The Garry Moore Show,* one skit featured her as a housewife who found a satchel of money. What twist did Moore and Durward Kirby arrange as a farewell ribbing?

5. At the end of *The Odd Couple*'s series run, what happened to Felix and Oscar?

6. The three Marx Brothers made their final appearance together in a 1959 episode of CBS's *General Electric Theater.* Who spoke the only line of dialogue?

7. At the end of their respective series, what common problem did the lead characters of *Mork and Mindy* and *The Time Tunnel* face?

8. How did Walter Cronkite close his news program?

9. How did Chet Huntley and David Brinkley close their news program?

10. What two young children appeared in the final half-hour episode of the *I Love Lucy* series?

11. What was special about the supporting characters appearing in the last episode of *Perry Mason,* "The Case of the Final Fadeout"?

12. As *The Dick Van Dyke Show* wrapped up its final season, most of the main characters signed up to work on a new (fictional) TV show. What was it based on?

13. In the final episodes of *The Mary Tyler Moore Show* and *The Bob Newhart Show,* the respective central casts went out singing. What two songs closed these shows?

14. At the end of the final episode of *Howdy Doody,* broadcast September 24, 1960, what did Clarabell the Clown do?

15. What was Dave Garroway's standard closing phrase for the *Today* show?

ANSWERS

1. *Skelton said in closing: "Good night, everyone. And may God bless. Good night."*

2. *John Charles Daly, moderator of the show.*

3. *Tuesday, August 29, 1967.*

4. *They changed the skit from the script Burnett had rehearsed, switching lines and entrance cues, and even altering props (such as jamming the zipper on the satchel). Burnett had to ad-lib before the audience from the original script to roll with these unexpected changes.*

5. *Felix remarried and moved back in with his wife, leaving Oscar to his old sloppy habits solo in the apartment.*

6. *"The Incredible Jewel Robbery" was performed in pantomime until the end of the story, when Groucho walked onto a police lineup, joined his brothers, and said that they wouldn't say a word until they had talked to their lawyer.*

7. *In both cases, the lead characters had traveled through time to another era and had not yet returned to their own time period when their respective series ended.*

8. *Before giving the day and date and saying good night, Walter Cronkite wrapped up the broadcast with the phrase, "And that's the way it is."*

9. *David Brinkley and Chet Huntley said to each other in turn: "Good-night, Chet." "Good-night, David." "And good-night from NBC news."*

10. *Lucie and Desi Arnaz, Jr., the real-life children of Lucille Ball and Desi Arnaz.*

11. *They included many of the production people that had worked on the series over the years, including Erle Stanley Gardner, creator of Perry Mason.*

12. *Rob Petrie's book, based on his life as a writer for a comedy-variety TV show. Actually, Rob had been writing the book for several seasons (a good reason for flashbacks) but was unable to land a publisher upon completion. Then Alan Brady stepped in and decided to turn the book into a television sitcom vehicle for himself, bringing along Buddy and Sally as writers and Mel Cooley as producer. This provided a clever in-joke ending to* The Dick Van Dyke Show, *because the program had been originally conceived by Carl Reiner (who played Alan Brady) as a sitcom vehicle for* himself, *a real-life writer for comedy-variety TV shows.*

13. The Mary Tyler Moore Show *ended with "It's A Long Way To Tipperary." One season later,* The Bob Newhart Show *wrapped up with "Oklahoma."*

14. *The normally silent clown looked directly into the camera and quietly spoke for the first time, saying, "Good-bye, kids."*

15. *Garroway would hold his hand up and say, "Peace."*

LAKEVIEW MIDDLE SCHOOL LIBRARY